Visitor'
TREASURE
ENG]

CW00640877

How To Use This Guide

This MPC *Visitor's Guide to the Treasure Houses of England* is designed to be as easy to use as possible. Each chapter is devoted to one of the eight houses covered, and are arranged south to north. MPC's distinctive margin symbols, the important places and points of interest printed in bold, and a comprehensive index enable the reader to find the most interesting places to visit with ease. In case you wish to extend your visit, at the end of each chapter, an Additional Information section gives details of other interesting attractions nearby, together with accommodation and dining out details. The area maps are designed to be of general interest to help you locate places mentioned in the text. They are not designed as route maps and motorists should always use a good road atlas.

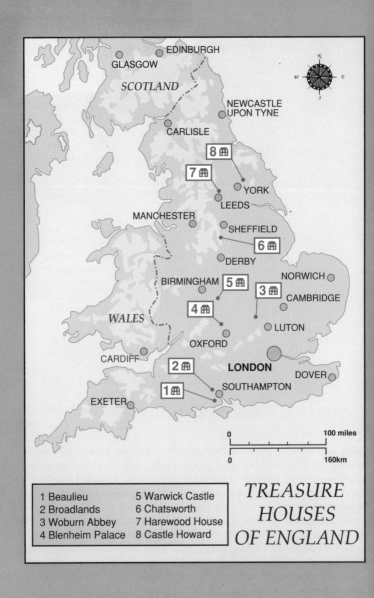

TREASURE
HOUSES
OF ENGLAND

1 Beaulieu
2 Broadlands
3 Woburn Abbey
4 Blenheim Palace
5 Warwick Castle
6 Chatsworth
7 Harewood House
8 Castle Howard

VISITOR'S GUIDE

TREASURE HOUSES OF
ENGLAND

John Barton & Lindsey Porter

MPC

HUNTER

Published by:
Moorland Publishing Co Ltd,
Moor Farm Road West, Ashbourne,
Derbyshire DE6 1HD England

ISBN 0 86190 306 4

Published in the USA by:
Hunter Publishing Inc,
300 Raritan Center Parkway, CN 94, Edison, NJ 08818

ISBN 1 55650 618 8 (USA)

British Library Cataloguing in Publication Data:
A catalogue record for this book is available from the British Library.

Colour origination by: P. & W. Graphics Pte Ltd, Singapore

Printed in Hong Kong by: Wing King Tong Co Ltd

Cover photograph: *Warwick Castle* (Warwick Castle)
Rear Cover: *Sèvres Vase, Harewood House* (Harewood House)
Page 3: *Charles Howard, 3rd Earl of Carlisle* (Castle Howard)

The illustrations have been supplied by:
Chris Andrews: pp79, 82, 83, 86, 87, 90, 91; Jeremy Barton: pp35, 43, 46, 50, 51, 70, 71, 79,
87; John Barton: pp19, 27; Broadlands (Lord Romsey): pp 35, 38; Castle Howard: pp171, 175,
178; Chatsworth: pp127, 130, 131; MPC: pp114, 123, 134, 135, 138, 139, 159, 182, 183;
Harewood House: pp146, 147, 151, 154, 155, 158; National Motor Museum Picture Library:
pp11, 14, 15, 22, 23, 26, 42; Three's Company: pp171, 174; Warwick Castle: pp99, 103, 106,
107, 110, 111; Tony Whittaker: pp167, 179; Woburn Abbey: pp55, 62, 63, 66, 67;

MPC Production Team:
Editorial: Tonya Monk
Design: Ashley Emery
Cartography: Alastair Morrison
Typesetting: Christine Haines

CONTENTS

Key to Symbols Used in Text Margin and on Maps

Recommended walks

Garden

Castle/Fortification

Other place of interest

Birdlife

Nature reserve/Animal interest

Church/Monastery/Ecclesiastical Site

Building of interest

Archaeological site

Museum/Art Gallery

Beautiful view/Scenery, Natural phenomenon

Parkland

Key to Area Maps

Motorway

Main Road

Minor Road

Railway

City

Town /Village

River/Lake

Airport

Key to House/Ground Plans

Park/Garden

Building

Point of Interest

Wall

Hedge

Tree

K Kitchen Shop

H Herb Shop

B Baby Care

G Gift Shop

Telephone

Toilets

Disabled Toilets

First Aid

i Tourist Information

INTRODUCTION

One of the most endearing aspects of England must be its villages. They conjure memories of age-old pubs by village greens, an ancient church nearby and a country house, peeping over a screen of trees and foliage. England lost over 2,000 country houses in the early years of the twentieth century. Today, the future for them is much brighter, for commercial uses can be found in many cases when domestic needs come to an end.

English country houses gave an outlet for a considerable wealth of talent: in architecture, decoration, furnishing and landscaping. The vast wealth created by the English aristocracy through Royal patronage (especially the disposal of monastic lands), rewards on the battle fields, investment in the arts, from commerce and from marrying 'well', enabled large sums to be spent, creating country seats of considerable importance.

Many of these still remain in the same families, or their descendants through marriage. Others came to the National Trust, either through death and arrangements with HM Treasury or through a commendable sense of duty in favour of national interest.

Fortunately, of the largest country houses, a group has remained virtually intact which represents some of the finest houses and the most valuable collections outside the Royal collection. This group is known as the Treasure Houses of England.

Palace House at **Beaulieu**, once the Great Gatehouse of Beaulieu Abbey, has been the ancestral home of Lord Montagu's family since 1538. It is also the home of the National Motor Museum, with over 200 cars, commercial vehicles and motor cycles.

Broadlands, where the Prince and Princess of Wales spent their honeymoon, houses many fine works of art and was also the home of the Earl Mountbatten of Burma, the Duke of Edinburgh's uncle.

Set in a 3,000-acre deer park, **Woburn Abbey** houses a magnificent collection of furniture, silver, porcelain and paintings. There are twenty-one Canalettos in one room, for instance. It also has nine different species of deer in its park and a 40-shop Antiques Centre.

Blenheim Palace, built for John Churchill by a grateful nation after the Battle of Blenheim in 1704, is also the birthplace of Sir Winston Churchill. Its Long Library alone houses 10,000 books and its State Rooms display tapestries, paintings, sculpture and fine furniture.

Situated in the heart of England is **Warwick Castle**, the finest medieval castle in England. William the Conqueror ordered the first castle to be built in 1068. Warwick Castle, sacked in 1264, besieged in 1642 and partly damaged by fire in 1871 remains to this day the most noble and picturesque of England's surviving ancient fortresses. The interiors date from the late seventeenth to the late nineteenth centuries, furnished in the grandest style. Warwick Castle, to this day, is the most visited stately home in Britain.

Chatsworth, in the Peak District National Park, houses perhaps the finest private collection in England outside the Royal palaces. The family wealth was founded in the sixteenth century by Bess of Hardwick who married four times and established one of the world's first vertically integrated industrial concerns involving coal and iron ore mining, smelting and marketing.

One of the finest collections of Chippendale furniture may be seen at **Harewood House**, which boasts one of our best Adam interiors. It was the home of the Princess Royal, the daughter of George V, while the grounds house over 150 different rhododendrons, many planted by the Princess Royal and her husband.

At **Castle Howard**, the collection includes paintings by Gainsborough, Holbein, Reynolds and Rubens. Its park is an example of the finest landscape architecture in Europe and the house also has an internationally famous collection of historical costume. The house was Sir John Vanbrugh's first work, completely breaking with architectural traditions.

All (except Warwick Castle) are family homes and all offer the prospect of a fulfilling day out in the country. Details on each house are accompanied by nearby attractions also worth visiting, plus accommodation in case you wish to extend your stay. John Barton is the author of the southern four houses and Lindsey Porter the author of the northern four. The houses are arranged from south to north.

It is hoped that you will enjoy visiting the Treasure Houses of England and that this book stimulates an interest in both other country houses and England's heritage in general.

This book is not intended as a substitute for the guide book to each house which in every case gives details of rooms and furnishings excluded here because of a lack of space.

1

BEAULIEU

The Abbey of St Mary at Beaulieu in Hampshire, founded in 1204 by King John, was the first Cistercian abbey established by an English king and the only abbey ever founded by that tyrannical monarch. King John had been persecuting the Cistercians and trying to extract taxes from them, and it was said that after having a nightmare in which he was beaten up by monks he decided to make amends by giving them money to build an abbey and also land in the New Forest on which to build it.

The rules of the Cistercian order stipulated that the sites of their abbeys should be remote and uncultivated. The site chosen for the abbey in the New Forest was ideal, at the head of a small navigable river and far from any other settlement. Peace and seclusion were assured and the site became known as Bellus Locus Regis, in Norman French Beaulieu, 'beautiful place'.

The Cistercian Order was founded in 1098 at Citeaux in Burgundy by St Robert; its members were known as 'white monks' because of their dress, perhaps chosen to symbolise their purity. Their first settlement in England was at Waverley, Surrey, in 1128. The Cistercian way of life in the twelfth century was extremely simple and austere, more so than that of the Benedictines from whom they had broken away. Poverty, chastity and silence were the basic rules by which they lived. They renounced all material possessions and refused all gifts from the outside world, from which they had totally withdrawn, except gifts of uncultivated land from which they could scratch a subsistence living. They even denied themselves 'luxuries' such as cloaks and warm bedclothes. Unlike other monastic orders they had no intellectual or cultural pursuits such as writing and illuminating manuscripts. Their days consisted of prayer, communal worship, work and meals, and they had very little privacy.

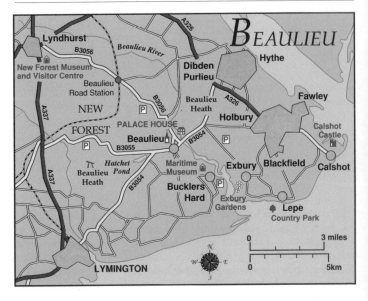

Cistercian churches, beautiful but austere, were devoid of the usual ornamentation and furnishings — stained glass, carvings, fine linen and embroidery. By the time Beaulieu was founded, however, Cistercian severity had relaxed a little. The monks now had winter as well as summer clothing, but the furnishings were still simpler than those in a Benedictine abbey.

The Order had officially banned new foundations in 1152, when there were about fifty Cistercian monasteries in England, but six more including Beaulieu were founded before the death of King John. Beaulieu was therefore a relatively late foundation and although not the last of the Cistercian abbeys it marked the end of an era of rapid growth.

A feature of the Cistercian Order was their use of Lay Brothers (*conversi*), recruited from all ranks of society, to do all the hard work — building, farming, shepherding, cooking. Books were forbidden to the Lay Brothers in order that they should remain illiterate. They lived apart from the monks in their own buildings and worked from sunrise to sunset. In spite of their hard life there was never any lack of recruits to their ranks, at least until the Black Death in the fourteenth century.

The Cistercians also introduced monastic 'granges' — large farmsteads in the outlying parts of their estates, supervised by a small

Beaulieu Abbey: the Lay Brothers' dormitory and cloisters

Beaulieu Palace House

staff of Lay Brothers. Beaulieu Abbey was allowed to pasture animals within the forest, even after it was forbidden to everybody else.
The English abbeys owned vast flocks of sheep; wool was the
foundation of England's wealth in the Middle Ages. The monks of
Beaulieu sold their wool to Italian merchants at Southampton (£16 a
sack for the best-quality wool).

Beaulieu was built originally to house thirty monks and a large
number of Lay Brothers. In 1329 there were thirty-six monks but at
the Dissolution of the Monasteries in 1538 there were only twenty-
one and no Lay Brothers, the land then being let to tenant farmers.
The accounts of Beaulieu Abbey survive for the period between 29
September 1269 and 28 September 1270 and are now in the British
Library. There were then seventy monks and about 140 Lay Brothers.
On the five monastic granges there were 4,000 sheep, and crops
grown included wheat, oats, rye, peas and beans. One-half of the
abbey's 8,600 acres was under arable; the cereal yield was ten bushels
per acre (today it is sixty).

There were 2,000 Cistercian barns in the Middle Ages and one of
the largest was at St Leonards, a few miles south of Beaulieu.
Remains of that barn and an adjacent chapel are incorporated in the
existing tithe barn, which is about one-quarter the size of the monastic barn. In 1269 Beaulieu Abbey had its own ship, the *Salvata*, also a
storehouse at Great Yarmouth and land as far away as The Lizard in
Cornwall. All the local inhabitants were connected with the abbey —
there was no separate village. Every night thirteen poor men were
fed and lodged in the guest house. The abbey precinct contained a
piggery, forge, tannery, shoemaker, parchment-maker, brewhouse
and a place for spinning and fulling wool. Fish were obtained from
three freshwater ponds and from the river, whose bed is still owned
by the manor, a legacy of monastic times.

Beaulieu Abbey Church was the largest Cistercian church in
England in area — 336ft (102m) long and 182ft (55m) wide across the
transepts. Winchester Cathedral is 556ft (170m) by 231ft (70m). It
took over 40 years to build and was dedicated in 1246 in the presence
of King Henry III. Building had slowed down after King John's death
for lack of money. The external building stone came from Binstead
in the Isle of Wight, the internal stone from Caen in Normandy and
the marble columns from Purbeck, Dorset, all of it transported up the
Beaulieu River to the abbey site. The plan of the church is carefully
preserved on the ground and visitors can appreciate its size by
walking round the foundations.

The nave had nine bays and the aisled apsidal chancel had ten
radiating chapels, a design based on the church at Clairvaux in

France. The transepts each had an eastern chapel containing three other chapels but the north transept had two aisles. The only parts of the church now standing above ground are the south aisle wall of the nave with its two cloister doorways, the west wall of the south transept and the night-stairs to the monks' dormitory. On the east side of the cloister the chapter-house entrance is easily recognisable; the chapter-house was square and had four piers. The west range of the abbey contained store-rooms and the Lay Brothers' quarters, which are now used to house a restaurant and the abbey exhibition. Of the monastic buildings south of the church the east range included a library/vestry, chapter-house, parlour and dormitory undercroft.

On the south side of the cloister is the monks' refectory, which is now the parish church of Beaulieu and is probably unique among English churches in being orientated north-south. In the west wall of the nave is the monastic pulpit from which readings were given to the monks at mealtimes; its former arcading has been replaced by Purbeck marble columns and the vaulting has been restored but the basic design survives. Monasteries had pulpits long before they were used in parish churches. The waggon roof of the nave is of an unusual design and dates from the fourteenth century. One respect in which this parish church is certainly unique is that entry is allowed only from the abbey/museum so visitors to the church must pay the full entrance fee.

Beaulieu Palace House

When the monasteries were dissolved by Henry VIII Beaulieu Abbey with its estate was sold in 1538 to Thomas Wriothesley, later first Earl of Southampton, for £1,340 (£1 for every 6 acres) and the abbot and monks were pensioned off. Wriothesley demolished all but four of the buildings and the stone was used to build Cowes, Hurst and Calshot castles. Only the inner gatehouse, outer gatehouse, refectory and west range were saved.

Soon after 1538 the inner or Great Gatehouse was converted to a small manor-house known as Palace House. Completed in the early or mid-fourteenth century, the gatehouse was not only unusually large but also strange in other ways. It had two storeys and was two bays deep, the inner bay being the gatehouse proper, and consisted of two parallel vaulted halls with two parallel chapels on the upper floor. The archways through which traffic passed are now filled in by windows. Medieval features still to be seen include wall arches, window tracery and the vaulting in the Lower Drawing-Room.

Not much is known of the history of the house in the second half of the sixteenth century. It remained in the ownership of the Wriothesleys for 129 years but was never their home, and it was let to the Chamberlain family in 1585 and to Sir William Oglander in 1590. Henry Wriothesley, the third Earl of Southampton, was the patron and friend of William Shakespeare, who dedicated two of his poems to him. King James I and King Charles I paid frequent visits to the house.

On the death of the fourth Earl in 1667 Beaulieu passed to his daughter Elizabeth, who married Ralph Montagu, later the first Duke of Montagu. Their son John, the second Duke, was responsible for the moat and the turrets, built as an anti-French invasion defence.

The Upper Drawing-Room of the Palace House was formerly a chapel

The Dining-Hall and table, made from a single elm tree

Towards the end of the eighteenth century Beaulieu came into the ownership of the Dukes of Buccleuch. In 1867 the estate was given by the fifth Duke as a wedding present to his son, Lord Henry Scott, who became the first Lord Montagu of Beaulieu and its first resident owner and was the grandfather of the present Lord Montagu.

The first Lord Montagu of Beaulieu decided to enlarge the house, which had not been altered since the early eighteenth century. The architect Sir Arthur Blomfield, a leading exponent of the Victorian Gothic style, carried out the alterations from 1871 to 1874. He retained the inner gatehouse as the central feature of the enlarged house, restored the south front to its original state and demolished and rebuilt the two north wings. Other alterations included a new main entrance on the west and the addition of an east wing, and many internal changes such as new fireplaces. The new house was a successful blending of the medieval Gothic and 'Scottish Baronial' styles.

A tour of the house is very informal — visitors are free to wander at their leisure through those rooms of the house that are always open, and there are guided tours of the private apartments when the family is not using them. The **Entrance Hall**, which in the nineteenth century was the billiard-room, is devoted to the life history of four generations of Montagus of Beaulieu, with family portraits and mementoes of their lives and travels. Delicate health obliged the first Lord to go abroad during the winter and the exhibits include items essential for travel in remote areas of the world at that time, such as a mid-nineteenth-century medicine chest complete with powders and pills.

The first Lord Montagu was the first owner of Palace House to live there permanently. His son, the second Lord, was a man of many skills — soldier, politician, author, sportsman, engine-driver and pioneer motorist. One of the exhibits is the inflatable waistcoat that saved his life when the S.S. *Persia* was torpedoed in 1915. He spent 36 hours in an open boat and when he arrived home he had the strange experience of reading his own obituaries.

The **Picture Gallery** (formerly the library) contains portraits of the owners of Beaulieu, including Thomas Wriothesley, Ralph, the first Duke of Montagu, who was the English Ambassador to France, and John, the second Duke of Montagu, an eccentric man of many talents who was once Master of the Ordnance and founded Montagu Town (now Bucklers Hard). There are also portraits of Royalty including King Charles II and the Duke of Monmouth, of whom the present Lord Montagu is a direct descendant.

The **Dinning Hall**, formerly the inner hall of the Great Gatehouse, was the family dining-hall until 1951 but is used now only on important occasions. The table was made from a single elm tree. The eighteenth-century plates are of pewter, a popular material then because it retained the heat. The room looks on to the fountain courtyard; the fountain is a representation of Triton with dolphins by Fleischmann.

The **Lower Drawing-Room** was originally the outer hall of the Great Gatehouse, and where guests were received, and is said to be haunted. The main drive once passed through the large outer arches and then through the arch where the fireplace stands. After the Dissolution it became the front hall of the house and then the dining-room. In this room on most days in the summer staff in period costume portray members of a nineteenth-century house party, an entertainment with piano and singing.

The **Corridor Gallery** contains photographs and documents relating to the family and the house and leads to the Victorian kitchen, furnished as it was in the nineteenth century, with contemporary tins, bottles, cutlery and utensils, a cast-iron range and a bell-board that summoned the servants.

On the first floor the **Coronation Room** or Ante-Room and the Private Dining-Room together formed one of the two chapels of the inner gatehouse. In the Coronation Room there are photographs of the Montagus in Coronation robes and Coronation admission cards. The **Private Dining-Room** was once the east end of the north chapel; it became a bedroom, then a sitting-room and since 1952 has been the main dining-room. The linenfold panelling came from the House of Commons after it was burnt down in 1834. The silver-gilt flagon, acquired in 1689, was probably part of the Coronation plate of Charles II in 1661.

The **Upper Drawing-Room**, which overlooks the village pond, was formerly one of the chapels and was possibly used by local people, who were not allowed into the monastery itself. The two chapels were divided by open archways, one of which was filled by a fireplace in the nineteenth-century restoration. One of the three pianos is a Broadwood dating from about 1818. This room is renowned for its psychic phenomena; Gregorian chanting is sometimes heard together with a smell of incense. The notice warning visitors of this adds that there is nothing to fear! The rooms shown on the tour of the private apartments include the Breakfast-Room, Drawing-Room, Picture Corridor and Library.

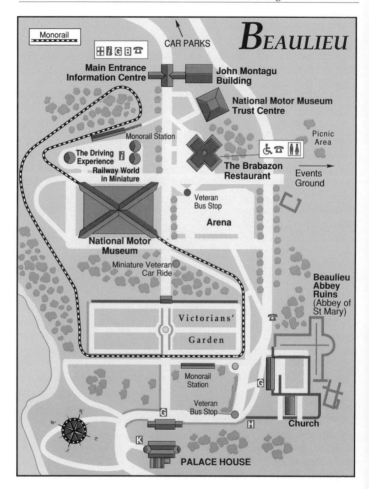

National Motor Museum

The Montagu Motor Museum (the National Motor Museum since 1972) began in a very small way, with five cars exhibited in the hall of Palace House when it was first opened to the public in 1952. It has grown over the last 40 years to become one of the two largest motor museums in Great Britain. It is now a charitable trust, founded to safeguard the collection for the nation, and its aim is to collect, preserve and exhibit vehicles, equipment and materials relating to the history of motoring in Great Britain. The museum owns over 300 vehicles although not all of them are on display at the same time.

Before making a tour of the museum visitors should go to the 'Wheels' exhibition and take a ride through motoring history. The 'Wheels' ride lasts about five minutes and the various set pieces and dioramas provide a social and historical background to the collection of vehicles in the museum.

The first motor car with an internal-combustion engine was driven by J. J. Lenoir in Paris in 1863; it ran on liquid hydrocarbon fuel. The German Nicholas Otto patented the four-stroke internal-combustion engine still used by vehicles today. The first successful petrol-engined car, built by Karl Benz in 1885 and demonstrated the next year, was a tricar with its engine driving the two rear wheels. A replica of the Benz tricar is in the museum. In 1886 Gottfried Daimler built the first four-wheeled petrol-engined car, powered by a more advanced type of engine than the Benz.

The first British petrol-driven cars were built by Frederick Bremer and J. H. Knight. Bremer's was first driven in December 1894, one month after the first imported car, a 2hp Benz Velo, took to the road

The National Motor Museum at Beaulieu reflects the history of the motor car

in Great Britain. Knight built only one car, originally a three-wheeler, later converted to four wheels, which is on display in the museum. Arnold, Lanchester and Austin cars followed soon afterwards.

In the first decade of motoring German and French cars predominated and nearly all the early cars in Great Britain were imported. Examples of these pioneer foreign cars in the museum include an 1898 Benz Velo, 1899 Fiat, 1899 Renault Voiturette, 1903 24hp De Dietrich tourer, 1903 60hp Mercedes (a beautiful and impressively solid car) and a 1903 De Dion Bouton, one of the five original cars in the museum. More De Dions were imported in the 1900s than any other make — 50 per cent of the cars on British roads were De Dions.

In 1896 the speed limit in Great Britain was raised from 4mph (6kph) to 12mph (19kph) and to celebrate this new law the first London to Brighton car run was held that year. Early British cars in the museum include an 1896 Arnold Dogcart (the first British firm to manufacture cars for sale — only two Arnolds survive), an 1896 Pennington Autocar (only five were made and sold for £157 each) and an 1897 Wolseley Dogcart (the second Wolseley to be built).

In the years before World War I famous names appeared on the motoring scene — Morris, Ford and Rolls-Royce. William Morris, a self-taught engineer who set up a cycle business at the age of 16, built his first car in 1912 and by 1914 had produced 1,300 Morris Oxford cars. Morris Motors was founded in 1919 and sales reached 63,000 in 1929, achieved by cutting costs to make the cars as cheap as possible.

Henry Ford built his first car in 1903. The famous Model T, which was introduced in October 1908, revolutionised the motor industry by its vast output. The Model T was first assembled in Great Britain in 1911 and by 1919 40 per cent of the cars on British roads were Model T Fords. The company's advert 'Any colour you like as long as it's black' was strictly correct, at least from 1914 to 1925. More than 15 million Model T Fords had been manufactured by 1927.

The Rolls-Royce Company was formed in 1906 and introduced the Silver Ghost, 'the best car in the world', which remained in production for 19 years. The 1909 Silver Ghost on display is perhaps the most distinctive car in the museum, and there is also a 1925 Phantom I, which replaced the Silver Ghost series.

Other cars of this period on view include a 1906 Renault (the first veteran car acquired by the Montagu Motor Museum), 1914 16hp Sunbeam, 1909 6hp Rover, 1909 8hp Humber (with a windscreen for the driver only), 1908 Unic taxi, 1912 Hispano-Suiza, 1914 'Prince Henry' Vauxhall and a 1915 'Prince Henry', one of only five surviving and a superb car of the veteran era. Veteran cars are those built before 31 December 1918, vintage cars those built between 1 January 1919 and 31 December 1930.

After World War I many more people could afford to buy a car when mass production lowered prices. Many small firms entered the market and at the 1920 Motor Show there were 149 British cars on display. Motor cars of the 1920s in the museum include a 1921 AC (cost £550), 1923 11.9hp Callcott, 1924 Delage DL, 1927 10hp Morgan Aero, 1928 14hp Bean (cost £365) and a 1924 Trojan, which could climb almost anywhere and whose engine had only seven moving parts — it cost £157 and prospective customers were asked 'Can you afford to walk?'

Family motoring was in full swing by the 1930s, aided by price competition and the introduction of the first £100 car — the 1931 Morris Minor, a two-seater with no bumpers and petrol consumption of 50mpg. The 1935 Model Y Ford was the first four-seater saloon to be sold for £100 — it was designed and developed in 5 months. Other cars of the 1930s in the museum include a 1935 Datsun (looking suspiciously like an Austin), 1935 Riley Falcon with preselector gearbox and sliding roof, 1938 Hillman Minx and a 1938 Morris 8.

After World War II came the age of mass motoring when nearly everybody who could afford a car felt it necessary to buy one. There were a million cars on British roads in 1930, 2 million in 1939, 9 million in 1965 and nearly 20 million in 1992. The famous Morris Minor was introduced in 1949 (price £359) and the equally popular Mini in 1959. Cars of the post-war period on display include a 1949 Ford Anglia, 1951 Standard Vanguard, Triumph Mayflower, 1962 Ford Cortina (an economical car that met with immediate success) and a 1953 Volkswagen 'Beetle', the best-selling car in history, surpassing even the Model T Ford.

The history of motor racing and land speed records cannot be divorced from ordinary motoring, because technical achievements and progress in the design of racing cars and sports cars helped to further the development of mass-produced cars. The first Grand Prix was held in 1906 and in the 1920s and 1930s large and powerful racing cars fought thrilling battles on the race-tracks of the world. In the 1920s Alfa-Romeo, Fiat, Sunbeam and Bugatti were supreme, and in the 1930s Mercedes and Auto Union. Since World War II Ferrari, Mercedes and the British Lotus and Cooper have had their days of triumph.

Racing cars and sports cars on display include a 1907 120hp Itala, 1903 Napier 'Gordon Bennett' (the oldest British racing car — maximum speed 75mph/120kph, 1924 Bugatti, 1930 4½-litre Bentley, 1933 Alfa Romeo (second at Le Mans 1935), 1928 Mercedes (once owned by Peter Ustinov), 1950 BRM V-16, 1954 Jaguar D-type (second at Le Mans 1954), 1967 Lotus 49, 1979 Ferrari and a 1988 McLaren. Land speed record-breakers in the museum include the 1920 350hp Sunbeam, 1927 1,000hp Sunbeam (Segrave 204mph/ 328kph), 1929 Golden Arrow (Segrave 231mph/372kph) and 1964 Bluebird (D. Campbell 403mph/649kph).

Commercial vehicles in the museum include a 1907 Gobron Brillié fire-engine, 1914 Ford Model T baker's van, 1913 Burrell showman's locomotive, 1924 Daimler in the shape of a Worthington bottle, 1935 Morris Commercial, 1937 Scammell Mechanical Horse, 1950 AEC RT double-decker bus and a 1922 Maxwell charabanc.

The motor-cycle gallery contains many classic and historic motor cycles, including a 1925 BSA B25 and a 1960 Norton Manx. The first motor cycle, a single-cylinder four-stroke, was built by Daimler in 1885, and the first production motor cycle was the 2½hp Motorrad, manufactured at Munich in 1894.

The BP Library of Motoring and the Kodak Motoring Picture Library in the John Montagu building at Beaulieu provide research and information services to motoring enthusiasts. The Library of Motoring holds several thousand books on motoring, a full range of old magazines and over 90,000 sales catalogues. The Picture Library holds over 200,000 black and white prints and colour transparencies, and in addition the Film Library holds 20,000 films and videotapes. The two Libraries are open during normal office hours.

Other attractions at Beaulieu include rides on an overhead mono-rail and on a replica 1912 London omnibus, a model railway and several children's amusements. Beaulieu village is charming and well-kept; ponies wander the streets and boats come up the river to the old mill. The Montagu Arms, Palace Lane, is the only hotel and inn in Beaulieu.

✳ Bucklers Hard

Bucklers Hard was first mentioned by name in the Beaulieu archives in 1698 and was probably named after a family called Buckle. There was no village then and not until 1724 was there an attempt to establish one near the river. In 1722 the second Duke of Montagu had financed an expedition to the West Indies to establish sugar planta-tions in St Lucia and St Vincent and he intended to build a small port on the Beaulieu River to import the sugar. The expedition failed and Montagu Town, as the port was to have been called, hung fire for 20 years. Then in the 1740s the site became an important shipbuilding centre and reverted to its old name of Bucklers Hard.

Bucklers Hard village, famous for shipbuilding in the eighteenth century

The New Inn, a recreation of village life at Bucklers Hard in 1793

Bucklers Hard had many advantages for shipbuilding. The river was never less than 5ft (2m) deep and much deeper at high tide, there was gravel on the bank to support launchways, the site was sheltered from the west winds and it was a safe distance from the river-mouth in case of war. Only one warship had ever been built on the Beaulieu River, the 48-gun *Salisbury* in 1698 at Bailey's Hard upstream of Bucklers Hard. The first warship to be completed at Bucklers Hard was the 24-gun *Surprise*, built by James Wyatt and launched in 1745.

Between 1745 and 1815 fifty-six naval vessels were built or rebuilt on the Beaulieu River, all but three of them at Bucklers Hard. After launching they were fitted out at Portsmouth. Nearly all of these ships were built by Henry Adams and his sons. Adams came to Bucklers Hard as Navy Board Overseer in 1744; in 1747 he resigned and took over the lease of the shipyard. His first vessel was the 24-gun *Mermaid*, launched in 1749, and over the next 45 years he established his reputation as a master shipbuilder by his skill as a craftsman, businessman and mathematician. Famous warships built by Adams included the *Agamemnon* (Nelson's favourite ship), *Indefatigable* and *Illustrious*.

As the shipbuilding yard grew so the number of houses in the village increased; there had been only six in 1740. In addition to the two rows of houses existing today (East Terrace and West Terrace) there were two other rows (Slab Row and Back Street), both demolished in the nineteenth century. In the late eighteenth century all the houses were owned by Beaulieu Manor but few of their tenants were employed by the manor; some worked at the shipyard and some at local farms. There was an inn (two from 1792) but Bucklers Hard was not a typical village. It had no church, school, doctor or local craftsmen; all these were at Beaulieu or Lymington. The houses flanking the village street were more substantial and comfortable than was usual in working-class houses of the mid-eighteenth century.

The Maritime Museum, opened in 1963, occupies the former New Inn and its extension. The exhibits illustrate the history of Bucklers Hard, especially in the eighteenth century when the village was a hive of industry. There are many fine models of the ships built here, including HMS *Euryalus* (1803) and HMS *Agamemnon* (1781), both of which fought at Trafalgar with another Bucklers Hard ship, HMS *Swiftsure* (1804). A copy of the log of the *Euryalus* shows the famous 'England expects… ' signal.

Other models include HMS *Kennington* (1756), HMS *Mermaid* (1749), HMS *Beaulieu* (1791), HMS *Illustrious* (1789) and HMS *Victory* (built at Chatham in 1765). Admiral Nelson's mementoes include his baby-clothes! Another strange exhibit is the Puckles gun, which was taken on the Duke of Montagu's expedition to the West Indies in the 1720s. An automatic weapon, it was designed to fire round bullets at Christians and square bullets at heathens. It was never fired in anger, perhaps because the firer could not determine the religion of his adversaries!

To give some idea of life at Bucklers Hard in the 1790s four domestic interiors have been re-created using local documentary evidence and knowledge of living conditions then. The reconstruction of the interior of the New Inn in 1793 is based mainly on drawings of contemporary inns and is peopled with known residents of the village. These include landlord Joseph Wort, Salt Officer Nicholas Cory, who assessed the tax on local salt production, blacksmith Richard Smith and shipyard foreman Henry Gill. The New Inn became an alehouse in about 1792, but there had been an inn at Bucklers Hard since 1742 (The Ship, now No 87 East Terrace). The inns were not just places for a quiet (or noisy) drink but served much the same purpose as modern village halls and community centres, all the business of the village being transacted there and all the local gossip passed round.

The interior of the labourer's cottage depicts the spartan life of a poorly-paid worker at that time. One downstairs room and two bedrooms were shared by a family of six. Meals were frugal but with a back garden they were able to keep chickens and grow vegetables and were not as badly fed as the labouring poor in the industrial towns. In West Terrace the shipwright's cottage indicates a rather better standard of living. A shipwright earned 20 to 30 shillings a week, about twice as much as a labourer, and could afford a few 'luxuries'. There are few reliable descriptions of contemporary working-class homes but these reconstructions are thought to be accurate representations of the period. Next door to the shipwright's cottage is the chapel, which was formerly a cobbler's shop, becoming the village school in about 1890 and later the Sunday school.

The fourth display is the Henry Adams room at the Master Builder's House Hotel, which can be viewed from an outside platform. Henry Adams is seen at his desk in 1779 consulting James Dann, the Navy Board Overseer. Henry Adams lived in this house from 1749 to 1805, and from this room could observe the work going on in the shipyard. Shipbuilding at Bucklers Hard ceased in about 1841. The census of that year recorded 26 farm labourers, 9 shipwrights, 2 fishermen and one or two other workers.

The master builder's house is now a hotel, restaurant and inn; there is also a café near the car-park. Parking on the public highway is forbidden from April to October. Cruises on the Beaulieu River on the motor-launch *Swiftsure* are available from Easter to September. An interesting walk of 2½ miles (4km) can be taken from the Montagu Arms in Beaulieu to Bucklers Hard or vice versa. From Beaulieu the footpath, which is part of the Solent Way long-distance path, passes Bailey's Hard, Keeping Copse, replanted about 1820 after it had been depleted for shipbuilding, and Bath Cottage, built in 1760. South of Bucklers Hard the Solent Way passes St Leonards Grange and the tithe barn, then follows by-roads to Lymington because there is no public access to the shore between Bucklers Hard and Lymington.

A model of Bucklers Hard village showing the construction of wooden men-of-wa

A beautiful sunlit glade in the New Forest

New Forest ponies

🌲 New Forest

In 1079 the New Forest became William the Conqueror's own private deer-park. Much less wooded than it is now and sparsely populated, it was mainly open heathland and had no oak, beech and coniferous trees so familiar today. Punitive laws protected the game in the forest and preserved it for the King's pleasure. The local inhabitants were allowed to graze their animals in the forest but it was found that this hindered the natural growth of the woodland. In the later Middle Ages therefore, when timber was needed for houses and ships, animals were banned from many parts of the forest, the first Enclosure Act being passed in 1482. The Forestry Commission now manages the forest for the Crown and conducts a profitable forestry business.

There are about 1,500 deer in the forest, most of them fallow deer with smaller numbers of red, roe, sika and muntjac deer. Red deer and fallow deer live in herds and can be seen if one is lucky almost anywhere in the forest. The smaller roe deer live in family groups, and although widely distributed are difficult to find. Sika deer inhabit the woods south of the railway line, and muntjacs are few in number and almost never seen. There is a deer sanctuary at Bolderwood where the animals come to feed.

There are also about 3,000 ponies, which belong to the commoners. Squirrels and rabbits are the commonest animals. Sometimes a fox may be seen in the remoter spots, and badgers emerge just before dusk from their setts. Stoats, weasels and hedgehogs are scarce. The only poisonous snake is the adder and even they rarely strike — spring is the dangerous time. Insects, particularly butterflies, abound. Most common birds can be seen and also rarer ones such as the heron, crossbill, woodcock and Dartford warbler, which is specially protected by law.

The oak is the typical tree of the forest and is widespread. It was much used in the eighteenth century for building ships. Beech is also common; some woods are predominantly beech and are especially beautiful in spring and autumn. There are two native birch trees, the silver and the downy. Conifers include Douglas fir, Norway spruce and Sitka spruce. Scots pine, which grows on the heathland, is not a native; it was introduced in 1776.

The New Forest is a largely unchanged medieval landscape, protected by special laws. Visitors are expected to obey certain rules, such as not feeding the animals, not lighting fires and not picking wild flowers. Many people get lost in the forest because they have no map. There are treacherous bogs in places — white cotton-grass is a danger sign. Near Beaulieu there are many access points to the New

Forest. The B3054 leads west to Hatchet Pond, a pleasant spot, and Hatchet Moor with its model aircraft flying area. On the B3056 to Lyndhurst there are several car-parks from which one can walk to the heart of the forest. The Solent Way follows the B3054 north-east across Beaulieu Heath, on which Bronze Age barrows are evidence of prehistoric occupation.

Exbury Gardens

Plant discoveries in Asia in the mid-nineteenth century opened up a new era in gardening in Great Britain. Until then rhododendrons were thought to be suitable only for large estates. In the seventeenth century only one rhododendron was cultivated in England (the 'Alpine rose'). By 1800 still only twelve species were known; by 1900 over 300 were known but that did not include the potentially richest source of all — inner China. There are now about 1,000 known species of rhododendron.

In 1919 the 2,600-acre Exbury estate was bought by Lionel de Rothschild and he moved into the house in 1922 from Inchmery, a mile away on the coast. He engaged a labour force of 150 men (in addition to his 75 regular gardeners) who in the next 10 years transformed the semi-wilderness into the gardens visitors see today. In addition to his 250 acres of rhododendrons he created an arboretum in which he aimed to collect a specimen of every tree that would grow in England. To offset the lack of rainfall he had boreholes sunk into underground springs.

In the 20 years between the wars Lionel de Rothschild created what is undoubtedly the finest rhododendron garden in the world, in that time introducing 462 new varieties. He died in 1942 and his son Edmund went to live at Inchmery. The arboretum became farmland but the rhododendron wood continued to flourish. Exbury is today a living memorial to its founder and a magnet for people who appreciate the beauty of rhododendrons and rock plants.

At **Lepe Country Park**, on the coast near Exbury, there is a good beach with safe bathing. Some of the Mulberry harbours used in the D-Day invasion were built there, and the remains of their construction site can be seen at Stansore Point. The Watch House on the shore was once a coastguard station from which smugglers could be observed entering the Beaulieu River.

Additional Information

Places to Visit

Beaulieu
Palace House and Gardens, National Motor Museum
Open: daily Easter to September 10am-6pm. October to Easter 10am-5pm.
Restaurant, gift shops, picnic area
☎ (0590) 612345
Directions: A326 and B3054 from Southampton. B3056 from Lyndhurst (entrance to Abbey and Museum on B3056). By rail to Brockenhurst then taxi, or train to Southampton, then by bus. Phone for details about special bus service.

Baby Care Room
Located adjacent to the Information Centre. Here mothers can attend to the needs of small children.

First Aid
Available from the Information Centre.

Information
About Beaulieu, the New Forest and the surrounding area can be obtained from the Information Centre.

Pass Outs
Are available from the admission turnstiles for use on the day of admission only.

Public Telephones
Located in the Information Centre, the Brabazon and next to the Abbey.

Wheelchairs and Pushchairs
A leaflet with helpful advise for visitors with pushchairs and wheelchairs is available from the Information Centre. Access for pushchairs is not possible in Palace House or 'Wheels' but they may be left alongside the entrance.

Dogs
Dogs are permitted in the grounds, but should be kept on a lead. Dogs are not allowed to be taken into the National Motor Museum, Palace House or on the Features. However, there is a special area beneath the Museum entrance where dogs may be left at owners risk.

Bucklers Hard
Maritime Museum
Open: daily Easter to Spring Bank Holiday 10am-6pm. Spring Bank Holiday to September 10am-9pm. October to Easter 10am-4.30pm.
River cruises: Easter to October
☎ (0590) 616203
Café (Easter to October), gift shop.
☎ (0590) 616246

Calshot
Calshot Castle
Open: daily Good Friday to September 10am-6pm.

Exbury
Exbury Gardens
Open: daily March to October 10am-5.30pm (or dusk).
Tea-room (March to October), gift shop and plant centre (all year).
☎ (0703) 891203

Lepe
Lepe Country Park
Open: dawn to dusk.
Restaurant, picnic areas.
☎ (0703) 899108

Lyndhurst
New Forest Museum & Visitor Centre
High Street
Open: daily from 10am. Closing time varies. Gift shop. Audio-visual theatre
☎ (0703) 283914

Tourist Information Centres

Beaulieu
John Montagu Building
Hampshire SO42 7ZN
☎ (0590) 612345, ext 278

Lyndhurst
New Forest Museum & Visitor
  Centre
Hampshire SO43 7NY
☎ (0703) 282269

Lymington
St Thomas Street car-park
☎ (0590) 672422
(summer only).

Accommodation and Eating Out

HOTELS

Beaulieu
Montagu Arms Hotel
Palace Lane
☎ (0590) 612324

Bucklers Hard
Master Builder's House Hotel
☎ (0590) 616253

Lyndhurst
Crown Hotel
High Street
☎ (0703) 282922

GUEST HOUSES

East Boldre
Westmoors
☎ (0590) 612435

Coolderry Cottage
Masseys Lane
☎ (0590) 612428

Lymington
Carters Farm House
Norleywood
☎ (0590) 65630

Beaulieu
Leygreen Farm House
Lyndhurst Road
☎ (0590) 612355

RESTAURANTS

Beaulieu
The Old Bakehouse
High Street
☎ (0590) 612777

Lyndhurst
Foresters
High Street
☎ (0703) 283601

Bucklers Hard
Master Builder's House Hotel
☎ (0590) 616253

2

BROADLANDS

The land just outside the town of Romsey known in 1541 as *Brodeland* had belonged to Romsey Abbey since before the Norman Conquest. The bailiff or tenant of the land probably had a house there but nothing is known about it. In 1544 after the Dissolution of the Monasteries the property was leased from King Henry VIII by John Foster (steward of the abbey) and Richard Marden for £900. On the accession of the young Edward VI Brodeland was granted to the King's uncle Sir Thomas Seymour, who quickly disposed of it to Francis Fleming. The latter built a comfortable Tudor mansion, the first house on the site of which there is any record. His daughter Frances married Edward St Barbe of Somerset and the property eventually passed into the ownership of the St Barbes for 117 years, during which time many alterations and improvements were made to the house. King James I stayed at the Tudor house on at least three occasions, and the mulberry trees in the walled garden are said to have been presented by him (or according to one source sold by him) to his host.

Celia Fiennes, a relation of the St Barbes, rode through England on horseback in the late seventeenth century and visited Broadlands in 1696. She described the house as a half Roman H in shape, with a large lofty hall in the middle, and projecting wings forming an open courtyard on the east side. The hall, which was divided in two by a staircase, occupied the whole width of the house. There was a gallery along the entire length of the house on the first floor giving access to 'handsome roomes'. On each wing there was a tower, one with a clock and the other with a sundial. The 'very fine' brick stable that she noted now houses the Mountbatten Exhibition. At the time of her visit Sir John St Barbe had recently completed some extensive alterations, mostly to the interior of the house, leaving the asymmetrical south and west fronts as they were. Parts of the old house still exist — the back staircase with its carved balusters and the Oak Room with its acanthus frieze and above the fireplace a carved frame to a Lely portrait in the style of Grinling Gibbons.

The last of the St Barbes left the property to his cousin Humphrey Sydenham, who never lived there. He in turn, ruined by the collapse of the South Sea Company, sold Broadlands in 1736 for £26,000 to Henry Temple, the first Viscount Palmerston.

Temple, whose father had property in Ireland, married Anne Houblon and was related to the first Governor of the Bank of England, and bought Broadlands as a second country seat. He soon removed the farmer who had rented the house, and his 'stinking yard', and promptly engaged the famous architect and landscape designer William Kent to improve the grounds by removing the old formal gardens. He made only minor alterations to the house during his occupation of it.

It was after the house came into the possession of his grandson the second Viscount in 1757 that the architectural history of the house we see today really begins. Broadlands is essentially the creation of the second Viscount, a retiring and unassuming man who had been on the traditional 'Grand Tour' of Europe on which he had absorbed the principles of Greek and Roman architecture, and fired with enthusiasm came home determined to apply them to his own house.

He made three trips to Italy and several to France, Germany and the Netherlands, and his knowledge and taste enabled him to choose the paintings, furniture and sculptures that make Broadlands such a Treasure House of art. He was a friend of Garrick, Reynolds, Johnson and Boswell and became a member of the Royal Society. He married twice; his first wife died only two years after their wedding. His Irish title allowed him to sit in the House of Commons as it did his Prime Minister son.

Palmerston engaged 'Capability' Brown, the country's foremost landscape designer, to alter and rebuild the house and redesign the park. He left the details of the house design to Brown after they had agreed the overall plan. The result of Brown's work is the beautiful Palladian mansion and its grounds so much admired today. Brown was not a particularly original architect, as evidenced by the resemblance of the west front at Broadlands to those of other houses designed by him, but as an incomparable landscape architect he was adept at blending the design of his houses with his chosen landscapes. Broadlands was one of Brown's most satisfying achievements and Palmerston was obviously well pleased with the redesigned house and park.

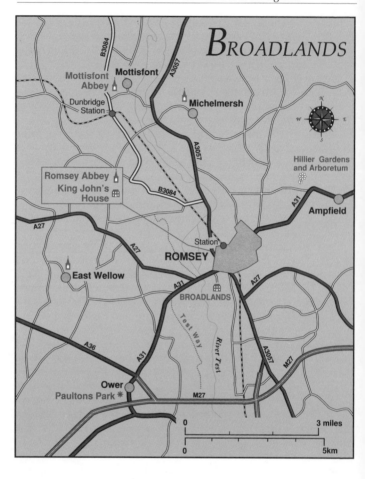

Brown started work on the house in March 1766 and finished it in 1774; he continued to work on the park and gardens until 1779. He built a new west range to replace the former irregular range facing the river and a new symmetrical south front, filling in most of the space between the wings with a complete east range. He also built the massive portico on the west front with its four Portland stone Ionic columns, a bold piece of architecture but eminently successful when seen as an integral part of the overall design of house and park overlooking the river. Brown's outdoor work included a 'greenhouse' (the orangery), kitchen garden, dairy and lodges. (The lodge

Broadlands, a house of mid-Georgian beauty

The Sculpture Hall

on the Southampton road was replaced by Nesfield in 1868). The final bill for the alterations to the house and grounds, more than £21,000, was presented to Palmerston by Brown in 1779.

Between 1788 and 1792 further major alterations were made to the house by the architect Henry Holland the younger, son-in-law and partner of Lancelot 'Capability' Brown. Palmerston wanted a larger dining-room and to accommodate it Holland increased the width of the south wing from two to three bays. In the interests of symmetry he did the same to the north wing, connecting the two wings with the recessed portico with four Ionic columns that forms the main feature of the present east front. This front was remodelled by T.L. Donaldson in 1859 — the quoins are his work. Holland also made alterations to Brown's rooms in the west range. In the Wedgwood Room he fitted bookcases at each end and a new chimney-piece of white and green marble. Lady Palmerston had a new suite of rooms for herself in the south-east corner of the house and filled them with furniture and souvenirs of her travels.

Henry John Temple, the third Viscount Palmerston, inherited Broadlands at the age of 17 in 1802. He was born at his father's town house in London and not as commonly believed at Broadlands, so he cannot be claimed as a Hampshire native but he spent much of his life at the house he loved. When he inherited Broadlands it had a mortgage of £10,000, which by 1817 had increased to £14,000. He paid off one-half of it by selling his house in Hanover Square, London. He sold some land at a profit to the Andover-Southampton Railway Company in 1856 and persuaded it to pay for the brick wall round the park. He became Secretary at War in 1809 at the age of 25, Foreign Secretary in 1830 and Prime Minister in 1855 at the time of the Crimean War.

Palmerston made a few alterations to the ground floor of the house including the doubling in size of the library. A one-storey extension was also built on to the north front and was used by Palmerston as a study; it was demolished in 1954. Sometimes he would travel on horseback from London to Romsey and sometimes by coach, but only after the coming of the railway to Southampton in 1840 and then to Romsey in 1847 could he visit Broadlands as often as he wished. He left the house for the last time in August 1865 and died in October, two days before his eighty-first birthday, still in office as Prime Minister. He was buried in Westminster Abbey.

On Palmerston's death the house passed to William Cowper, later Lord Mount Temple, the younger of Palmerston's two stepsons. On his death in 1888 there was again no male heir; the house became the property of Evelyn Ashley, the second son of Lord Shaftesbury, brother-in-law of Lord Mount Temple. Ashley's son Wilfrid married the daughter of the wealthy Sir Ernest Cassel, and their daughter Edwina, wife of Earl Mountbatten, inherited Broadlands in 1939. She died in 1960 and Earl Mountbatten died in 1979, when the property passed to Lord Romsey, the eldest son and heir of Patricia, elder daughter of Earl Mountbatten, who inherited her father's title and is

Countess Mountbatten. Broadlands was opened to the public for the first time on 19 May 1979.

So much for the history of the building and its owners. It is best to recount the history of the interior and its contents in the order in which visitors view the rooms on a guided tour. The main entrance to the house is through the loggia on the east front. The Domed *Entrance Hall*, designed by Holland the younger, links the entrance with the Sculpture Hall (originally the lower part of the Great Hall of the Jacobean house), which lies immediately behind the Saloon in the west range and is the least altered of Brown's rooms. The Roman Doric screen at one end disguises the asymmetry of the **Sculpture Hall** and serves as a setting for the antiquities collected by the second Viscount on his Grand Tour. His portrait with his plan of the Temple of Paestum was painted in Rome by Angelica Kauffman. In Italy in 1764 he spent over £500 on statues and carvings. This fine collection includes a panel of the early third century depicting a boar-hunt and a marble carving of a boy on a dolphin by Joseph Nollekens, the famous eighteenth-century British sculptor.

The **Dining-Room** was executed by Holland in 1788 (his drawing for the ceiling survives) but Palmerston supervised every detail in this room. The life-size Van Dyck paintings bought by Sir Ernest Cassel are of Charles I, Henrietta Maria and Madam Vinck; the painting *The Itinerant Musician* bought by the second Viscount in Paris in 1773 is by an unknown artist. The painting by J.B. Monnoyer above the sideboard was given to Palmerston by Joshua Reynolds in 1790. Its original wreath of flowers remains. A picture of Roman Charity was in the centre. This was painted over by Reynolds with an allegorical hand and eye. Palmerston disliked this strange subject and with Reynolds' permission commissioned Thomas Lawrence to replace this with a portrait of Lady Hamilton. The eighteenth-century mahogany sideboard was made specially for the Dining-Room.

The **Saloon**, situated behind the west portico, has an elaborate neo-Classical ceiling, which like those in the Drawing-Room and the Wedgwood Room dates from the 'Capability' Brown period and was probably designed and executed by Joseph Rose the elder. The delicate white and gold plasterwork was also by Rose, who had worked for Robert Adam and was described as 'the first man in the Kingdom as a plasterer'. Much of the ceiling and plasterwork has been replaced after dry rot but the new work is virtually indistinguishable from the original. Holland's alterations were confined to redecoration, as in the Drawing-Room. The white marble chimney-piece and the overmantel were probably substituted by Holland in

The elegant interior of the Saloon

The unique collection of Wedgwood pottery as seen in the Wedgwood Room

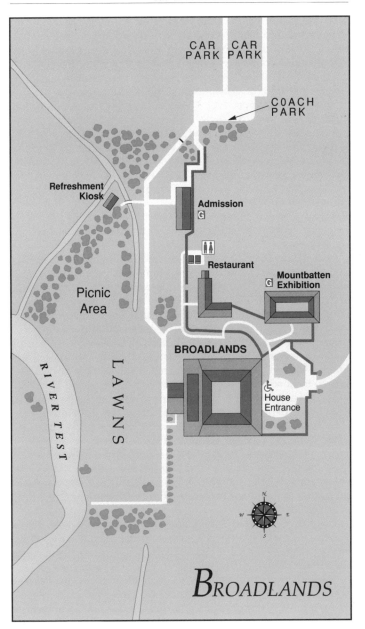

1788. In the nineteenth century one of the recesses was lined with mirrors and the other one was given double doors to the Drawing-Room. In World War II this room was used as a hospital ward (Broadlands became part of the Royal South Hants Hospital) and since then it has been used for receptions, with famous musicians such as Sir Malcolm Sargent providing the entertainment.

The **Drawing-Room**, which visitors can view from the doorway but may not enter, is the centre of family life at Broadlands. The oval paintings on the ceiling, including those of Venus, Cupid and the three Graces, have been attributed to Angelica Kauffman. The chimney-piece was moved here from the Wedgwood Room by Holland and the carpet was designed by David Hicks, husband of Earl Mountbatten's younger daughter Pamela, to mirror the ceiling. The eighteenth- and nineteenth-century portraits are by Reynolds, Romney, Raeburn, Hoppner and Lawrence. The room as a whole displays a skilful blending of modern comfort with eighteenth-century elegance.

In the **Wedgwood Room** the style of the decorations is reminiscent of the famous pottery designs; the ceiling and frieze were executed by Rose in 1869 and the bookcases, wall decorations, chimney pieces and mirrors are all by Holland. His wall decorations were in bolder relief to compliment Rose's existing ceiling and frieze. Some of the Wedgwood pieces were bought by the second Viscount Palmerston in the 1780s and 1790s and others by Lord Mount Temple early in the twentieth century. There are four portraits by Lely, including one of Frances Stewart, Duchess of Richmond, who was chosen by Charles II to be the model for the figure of Britannia on his coins. This room was also a hospital ward during when the walls and bookcases were boarded up to prevent damage. It is used now by the family for tea.

Upstairs the **Oak Room** was once part of the two-storey Great Hall of the Tudor house; the Sculpture Hall is directly underneath it. Before the east portico was built the room enjoyed an outlook over the park; it is now used by Lord Romsey as a cinema. The two red chairs with the Prince of Wales feathers in the Oak Room were used for guests at the investiture of the Prince of Wales at Caernarfon Castle in 1968.

The bedrooms on the first floor have accommodated many distinguished visitors, including the present Royal Family. Princess Elizabeth and Prince Philip, and Prince Charles and Princess Diana, began their honeymoons at Broadlands.

The Jacobean spiral staircase leads down to the **Ships Passage** where models of ships on which Mountbatten served are displayed. The World War I ships have, as a background, panoramas of the Firth of Forth, Spithead and Portsmouth, and the World War II ships have one of Grand Harbour, Malta. The last two rooms on the tour are the **Palmerston Room**, which contains a desk at which the Prime Minister stood when working and a portrait of him on horseback at Westminster, and the **Gun Room**, which contains a collection of Stubb's prints above the fireplace and a collection of Earl Mountbatten's walking sticks.

Mountbatten Exhibition   ✳

The Mountbatten Exhibition is housed in the old stable building, which dates from the late seventeenth century when the St Barbe house was still standing. The Exhibition presents in great detail the life history of one of the most colourful personalities of the twentieth century, a man who gave invaluable service to his country in peace and war, and whose leadership and determination in World War II contributed in no small measure to the Allied victory.

Lord Louis Mountbatten was born in 1900, the younger son of Prince Louis of Battenberg and Princess Victoria of Hesse, granddaughter of Queen Victoria, who was his godmother. His family in 1917 decided it would be tactful to drop its German name. Lord Louis joined the Royal Navy in 1913 and served two years at sea in World War I. After the war he studied at Cambridge University and soon afterwards accompanied his cousin Edward, Prince of Wales, on tours to Australia, New Zealand, India and the Far East. In India he met his future wife, Edwina Ashley, daughter of Lord Mount Temple, and their marriage in 1922 was the society wedding of the year. One of the items in the Exhibition is the bride's wedding head-dress.

Louis Mountbatten was an expert in wireless communication; he invented several devices for the Royal Navy and wrote two handbooks on the subject. He was captain of the Royal Navy polo team and wrote a best-selling book on the game. His first sea command was of HMS *Daring* in 1934 which was lost in 1940 on convoy duties after Mountbatten had been transferred to the more famous HMS *Kelly*. In 1942 he was appointed Chief of Combined Operations, an important post for a young officer, and became a member of the Chiefs of Staff Committee. He helped in the planning that led up to the successful invasion of Europe in 1944, but before D-Day arrived he had been appointed Supreme Allied Commander in south-east Asia with the acting rank of admiral, the youngest in the history of the Royal Navy.

Mountbatten had the agreeable task of accepting the surrender of the Japanese forces; the instrument of surrender and the surrender sword are on display in the Exhibition. His responsibilities were not finished with the end of the war for soon afterwards he was appointed the last Viceroy of India and in 1947 after the transfer of power he became the Governor-General of India. He then resumed his naval career and in 1955 became First Sea Lord, as his father had been from 1912 to 1914. In 1965 he retired from active duty after more than 50 years of service but continued to perform many official duties and pursue many interests, and was now able to spend more time at Broadlands. The nation was deeply shocked when in 1979 he was assassinated in the Republic of Ireland by the IRA.

In the Exhibition's cinema a 25-minute film of Mountbatten's life highlights his major achievements in peace and war. The 1924 Rolls-Royce Silver Ghost 40/50 Cabriolet on display was Mountbatten's second Rolls-Royce; it has been restored by the National Motor Museum at Beaulieu. There is also a 150mm Japanese gun captured in Burma by an Indian division of the 14th Army.

Broadlands has an atmosphere markedly different from that at some of the country's stately homes. There is no overt commercialisation; visitors will feel they have been invited by personal guests to

A 1924 Rolls-Royce Silver Ghost, once owned by Earl Mountbatten and now on display in the Stableyard at Broadlands

view the house. Indeed you do not become aware of the house until after leaving the visitors' reception area in the old dairy and then catching sight of the west front and the lawn sloping down to the River Test. Broadlands offers a friendly, informal welcome to its visitors.

Romsey ❋

The town of Romsey lies on gravel terraces that separate several small streams flowing parallel to and then into the River Test. There was a Romano-British settlement here but there is no evidence of continuous occupation from Roman to Saxon times. After the founding of the abbey in AD907 and its refounding in AD967 most of the town and the fields east of the Test were owned by the abbess, who was the virtual ruler of the local community. By the time of the Norman Conquest there was a flourishing settlement around the abbey. The nuns had pupils and guests, many of them from wealthy families, and the influx of money benefited local traders. There were fifty-four nuns in 1030; after the Conquest the problem was one of too

Romsey Abbey

many nuns and after the Black Death of too few (there were only twenty-one in 1492).

Early in the twelfth century the abbey was granted a market in the town every Sunday and a yearly four-day fair by Henry I; and a second fair was granted by Henry III in 1272. After the Black Death the abbey's power and wealth declined. Nevertheless Romsey remained a prosperous market town, sending woollen cloth and leather to Southampton in exchange for essential goods and raw materials for local industries. Tanning was important throughout the Middle Ages, indeed right up to modern times. The main source of the town's wealth was the processing of wool and cloth in the local mills.

When the abbey was dissolved the townspeople, in particular the wealthy ones, raised £100 to buy the abbey church from the King, a lucky escape from demolition made possible only because the north aisle and north transept had been used for a long time as the parish church. Included in the sale were the processional way around the church and land for the cemetery, but not the six church bells, which had already been removed and sold. The town survived the Dissolution of the abbey and in 1544 acquired one of the largest parish churches in England.

The economic effects of the suppression could have been serious, for many of the townspeople had relied on the abbey for their livelihood, if the flourishing market and established trades had not existed.

In 1607, exactly 900 years after the founding of the abbey, Romsey received its charter of incorporation, which made possible the appointment of a mayor, six aldermen and twelve burgesses. During the Civil War the town was plundered at least once by each side. There is a notice on the Conservative Club in the Market Place stating that two of Cromwell's soldiers were hanged from the bracket on the wall — the building was the Swan Inn in those days. By 1760 the cloth trade had declined. Romsey still profited by its market and did not stagnate like some other small towns, continuing with trades and manufactures, such as paper-making, grain-milling, sack-making, brewing and tanning. By the mid-nineteenth century brewing became the most important.

Before the Dissolution therefore the history and fortunes of Romsey were inseparable from those of the abbey. Founded as a Benedictine nunnery in AD907 by King Edward the Elder for his daughter Ethelflaeda, the abbey was refounded by King Edgar in AD967. Recent evidence suggests that the first nunnery was established within a pre-existing parochial minster. There was certainly a church immediately prior to the present one; the foundations of the apse of a Saxon church found beneath the present nave have been preserved and left exposed for the benefit of visitors. That the town was subordinate to the abbey in the Middle Ages is suggested by the fact that there was then no separate parish church, the inhabitants having to use part of the abbey church. At the Dissolution the church was sold to the town; the bill of sale is displayed in the church and for £100 it must represent one of the best bargains ever obtained from a king of England, certainly from Henry VIII.

The church is one of the finest Norman buildings in the country and its architecture is the most impressive of all England's Roman-esque abbey churches and surviving medieval nuns' churches. It was begun in about 1120 and extended in the thirteenth century. The earliest parts of the church are the choir, transepts, ambulatory and tower, dating from 1120-50. In the nave the Norman eastern bays of 1150-80 contrast with the Early English western bays of 1230 to 1250, yet the two styles of architecture make a most satisfying and impres-sive composition, perfectly proportioned. It is not known how many bays the eleventh-century church had — evidence suggests five in the nave and three in the presbytery, which would have made it unusually short for a typical Benedictine church, which usually had about eleven bays. The eastern end at Romsey was probably a square version of the Benedictine apse and ambulatory design, and may have been the earliest of its kind.

The nave and chancel are broad and spacious. The shafted piers extending up to the arches of the triforium give the nave an impres-sion of great height, emphasised by the single shafts extending up to the clerestory. There is one circular pier on each side between the first two bays. At Romsey there was no transitional style between the Norman and Early English, and the progress of the building can be deduced from the junctions of the two styles. The clerestory was the last part to be constructed, the south side before the north. In the clerestory the Early English style starts at half a bay from the crossing tower, and in the gallery at the arches of the third and fourth bays.

There are two relics of the Saxon period, one inside and one outside the church. The rood or crucifix behind the altar in the south aisle chapel dates from about AD1000 and shows Christ on the cross (the Tree of Life) with Mary and John on either side, angels with censers on the arms of the cross, and Longinus and a soldier below. The rood on the outside west wall of the south transept is much larger. This priceless artistic relic dates from the eleventh century and depicts Christ with his arms outstretched and the hand of God appearing from a cloud.

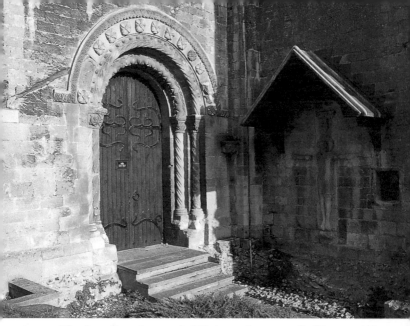

The eleventh-century rood of Christ on the west wall of Romsey Abbey

The Market Place in the heart of Romsey

There are many other interesting things to see in the church, including in the south transept the grave of Earl Mountbatten. Nearby is a memorial to Sir John St Barbe of Broadlands and his wife with the inscription 'Be in shares, in blest glorie', which is supposedly an anagram of their names, but close examination reveals that two letters are incorrect. Also in the south transept is a thirteenth-century Purbeck marble effigy of a lady wearing a wimple; the canopy above it with its ogee arch, however, is fourteenth century. At the west end of the nave is the tomb of Sir William Petty, who was born in Romsey in 1623 and was a founder-member of the Royal Society.

There was once a Lady Chapel at the east end of the church but it was destroyed at the Dissolution. In the retrochoir the two chapels are dedicated to St Mary and St Ethelflaeda — as is the abbey church itself. In St Mary's Chapel there is a twelfth-century wall-painting, during restoration of which in 1976 a strange discovery was made. Embedded in the wall were remains of some allium bulbs, believed to be the oldest botanical specimens in Europe. Known as the 'Romsey Rose', they can be seen in the Treasury in the south choir aisle.

The chapel of St George is at the east end of the north choir aisle; in front of the altar there are tiles depicting the Crusades. In the aisle is the only surviving piece of needlework by the Romsey nuns, dating from the fifteenth century and made probably from two similar green velvet copes. The nuns of Romsey and other abbeys were renowned for their needlework.

The beautiful Decorated windows at the east end of the church date from 1270. The stained glass in the central window is dedicated to one of the owners of Broadlands, William Cowper Temple (1811-1888). 'He served his country in Parliament 53 years and his God through life, doing good to men, and walking blameless before the Lord.' Other windows at the east end and in the south transept are in memory of Broadlands families. Towards the eastern end of the north aisle is a monument by Fuchs of Mrs Maud Ashley who died in 1913. In immaculate white marble, she is shown with her two young daughters. The elder is Edwina who married Lord Mountbatten. Under the west window are three Palmerston family tablets. Nearby are two flags given by Lord Mountbatten. One is his personal flag as Supreme Allied Commander of south-east Asia in Singapore, 1945, and the other flown in Delhi in 1947 when he was the last Viceroy of India. Over the high altar below them is a bas-relief of the Madonna and Child; there are six other altars in the church, each of which is used once a week for Holy Communion.

Before the Dissolution the north transept was used at the chancel of the parish church, and in its west wall can be seen the arch that led to an extra aisle, now demolished. There is a rare painted wooden reredos dating from about 1525; it depicts a row of saints with Christ rising from the tomb. A window in the chapel in this transept commemorates the Reverend Berthon, a nineteenth-century vicar of Romsey who was also a famous inventor. In 1849 he designed and built a life-saving collapsible boat. In the choir is the Mountbatten family pew and a fine Victorian organ, one of the best surviving examples from the great period of English organ-building.

The glories of Romsey Abbey tend to overshadow other buildings of historical interest in the town, but there is much to be seen by an observant visitor. The Market Place is the very heart of Romsey, and lies close to the east end of the abbey. Originally it was much larger. The corner occupied by the Victorian Town Hall, and the island block with its classically styled Corn Exchange, are both intrusions. In the centre stands a fine bronze statue of the third Viscount Palmerston, posed as he often stood addressing Parliament. Around the Market Place the eighteenth- and nineteenth-century façades hide many older oak-framed structures, such as the White Horse and the Dolphin, two of the hostelries dating back to the age of the stage-coach. On this triangular Market Place converge the three main roads, The Hundred, Bell Street and Church Street.

 King John's House near the abbey in Church Street is a first-floor hall- house built in the mid-thirteenth century, in a remarkable state of preservation. In 1927 when it was discovered to be so old it was thought to be King John's Hunting Box. It was a guest-house for nobility visiting the neighbourhood. The upper floor was the living and sleeping area and the medieval plaster carries scratched graffiti, including a caricature of Edward I. Downstairs part of the floor is cobbled, using bones of cattle, and is late seventeenth century. Attached to King John's House is the timbered-framed Tudor Cottage, dating from the mid-sixteenth century. At number 28-32 Church Street a plaque records that in 1623 Sir William Petty was born in a previous house on the site. He was an economist, anatomist, inventor and cartographer and Pepys described him as 'one of the most rational men that ever I heard'. Charles II said of him: 'he is not contented to be excellent, he is always aiming at impossible things'. A plaque in Bell Street records the passage of King William Rufus's body to Winchester after his mysterious death in the New Forest.

Visitors interested in canals can follow on foot a stretch of the old Andover Canal north of Romsey, from the former Plaza cinema to the village of Timsbury. Constructed in 1794, the canal was used for a time in transporting heavy goods to and from Southampton and Andover but was superseded by the railway when the Eastleigh line opened in 1847 and the Southampton line in 1865. Palmerston gave some land for the second railway line and asked for the main Southampton road to be resited further away from Broadlands. Until then the road had left Romsey by what is now Palmerston Street and had gone straight through Broadlands Park. The Test Way long-distance footpath passes to the west of Romsey and walkers using it can leave it at Middle Bridge in order to visit Broadlands or explore the town.

East Wellow Church

East Wellow Church, a few miles west of Romsey, is difficult to find without a map, but a visit will prove well worth while. In the churchyard is the grave of Florence Nightingale, who died in London at the age of 90 and in obedience to her wishes was buried here in the family grave. She lived at nearby Embley Park when she was a child. The grave is marked by an obelisk with her initials 'F. N.'. The church is noted for its thirteenth-century wall-paintings, which although not very well preserved are recognisable as St Christopher holding a child in his arms, the murder of Thomas á Becket and a scene from the life of St Margaret of Antioch, to whom the church is dedicated. There are also Jacobean stalls, a carved pulpit and a few mementoes of the life of Florence Nightingale.

Mottisfont Abbey, Hillier Gardens and Paultons Park

A few miles north of Romsey in the Test Valley is **Mottisfont Abbey**, a house owned by the National Trust. The Augustinian priory established here in the thirteenth century was dissolved in 1536 and the priory and its lands were given to Lord Sandys of The Vyne in exchange for the villages of Chelsea and Paddington. He transformed the nave of the abbey church into a Tudor mansion; the north front of the present house is the north wall of the former church nave. In the eighteenth century the house was again altered and its south front of mellow brick and stone quoins dates from then. On the east front of the house there is a pointed arch that once led from a chapel into the south transept. Mottisfont Abbey enjoys one of the most beautiful situations of any country house in England, shaded by giant trees with the River Test flowing past the east front.

Only two rooms are open to visitors, who are admitted strictly in order of arrival by timed ticket (Tuesday, Wednesday and Sunday 1-5pm only). One of the rooms is the Saloon or Drawing-Room, which was decorated in 1938 by Rex Whistler, his last and greatest work. The room as a whole is an astonishing piece of Gothick fantasy, with its simulated stucco ceiling and painted colonnettes. The other room open to visitors is the monks' cellarium. The famous garden at Mottisfont Abbey contains the National Trust's collection of roses, which are at their best in June. In the eighteenth century most large houses had an ice-house in the grounds in which to store ice, and there is one here open to view.

Mottisfont parish church was once attached to the bishopric of York and dates from the mid-twelfth century. There is more fifteenth-century stained glass here than in any other church in Hampshire. The monument of 1584 depicting an unknown Elizabethan kneeling family, an early example of this type of monument, has Renaissance details. The church has a fine Norman chancel arch and a bell-tower supported by six timber posts.

Not far away on the other side of the River Test is the village of **Michelmersh**, where the parish church has an unusual detached weatherboarded tower of uncertain date. There are some interesting

Mottisfont Abbey enjoys one of the most tranquil settings of any country house in England

memorials in the church, one of them an effigy of a crusader knight with a stag at his feet. The memorial to Trustram Fantleroy of 1538 is probably the earliest example in Hampshire of one with detached kneeling figures. The field south of the church is said to have been the one where 600 knights and archers gathered in 1415 on their way to the Battle of Agincourt.

The **Hillier Gardens** and Arboretum, 2½ miles (4km) north-east of Romsey, near Ampfield, has one of the largest collections of trees and plants in Europe. It has the most complete collection of 'woody' plants in the country (10,000 species and varieties) and 3,000 species of trees. The best time for a visit is in April or May.

At **Ower**, 2 miles (3km) south-west of Romsey, **Paultons Park** offers adults and children a wide range of attractions. The park has been reclaimed from a derelict lake and gardens and boasts the largest privately-owned collection of wildfowl in the south of England. In addition to the usual amusements for young children there are aviaries, gardens and two museums. The Romany Museum shows the way of life of gypsies through the ages and has a large collection of living-wagons, and the village life museum has replicas of a wheelwright's shop, a blacksmith's shop and a dairy.

The picturesque Test Valley

Additional Information

Places to Visit

Broadlands
Open: Easter to September:
Saturday to Thursday 12noon-4pm.
August daily. Tea room, gift shop,
picnic area. Accompanied children
under 12 free. Special rates for parties.
☎ (0794) 516878
Directions: On M27 leave at
Junction 3: A3057 to Romsey. A31
from Winchester and Ringwood.
By rail, Southampton to change for
Romsey, Entrance to house on A31.

Ampfield
Hillier Gardens and Arboretum
Open: Monday to Friday 10.30am-
5pm (all year). Saturday, Sunday,
Bank Holidays 10.30am-6pm
(March to November). Closed
winter Saturdays. 10.30am-dusk
(December to February).
Tea-room (March to November),
picnic area.
☎ (0794) 68787

Farley Mount
Farley Mount Country Park
3 miles (5km) west of Winchester.
Open: dawn till dusk.
Nature trails, picnic tables.

Mottisfont
Mottisfont Abbey
Open: April to October
House: Tuesday, Wednesday and
Sunday 1-5pm.
Garden: Saturday to Wednesday
12noon-6pm. Rose garden also
open during season on Tuesday,
Wednesday, Thursday, Sunday 7-
9pm. Gift shop.
☎ (0794) 40757 or 41220

Ower
Paultons Park
Open: daily mid-March to October,
10am-6.30pm. (Earlier closing in
spring and autumn).
Restaurant, tea-room, gift shops.
☎ (0703) 814442

Romsey
Romsey Abbey
Open: daily 7.30am-6pm.

King John's House
Open: Spring Bank Holiday to
September: Tuesday to Saturday
10.30am-12.30pm. Monday to
Saturday 2-4pm. April, May,
October: Saturday 2-4pm.
☎ (0794) 512200

Tourist Information Centres

Romsey
Bus Station Car-Park
Broadwater Road, S05 8BF
☎ (0794) 512987 (summer only)
Open: 9.30am-5pm Easter to October.
10am-3.30pm November to Easter.

Southampton
Above Bar, S09 4XF
☎ (0703) 221106

Accommodation and Eating Out

HOTELS

Romsey
Abbey Hotel
Church Street ☎ (0794) 513360

White Horse Hotel
Market Place ☎ (0794) 512431

RESTAURANTS

Ampfield
Potters Heron Hotel
Winchester Road ☎ (0703) 266611

Romsey
Old Manor House
Palmerston Street ☎ (0794) 517353

3

WOBURN ABBEY

Woburn was first mentioned by name in a charter of King Edgar in AD969 relating to the grant of Aspley. The name 'Woburn, was derived from the Old English words '*woh*' and '*burna*' meaning 'crooked or winding stream'. At the time of Domesday Book the manor of Woburn was held by Walter Giffard, who let it to a tenant; it then included 2,400 acres of arable land, 800 of which were cultivated.

In 1145 the Cistercian abbey of St Mary was founded at Woburn by monks from Fountains Abbey in Yorkshire. It occupied the same site as the present house, was sheltered on three sides by hills and trees and enjoyed a wide view to the west. The abbot became the lord of the manor and in 1242 King Henry III granted him the right to hold a weekly market on Fridays 'at the chapel of old Woburn' and a three-day fair in September. The village, situated at the gates of the abbey, began to prosper. The parish church was at Birchmore, just outside the present village. The abbey had two granges, Whitnoe and Utcote. There is still an Utcoate Grange on the Leighton Buzzard road.

Little is known about Woburn and its abbey in the fourteenth and fifteenth centuries. Two more fairs were granted in 1530, and in 1538 Henry VIII's commissioners came to Woburn at the time of the Dissolution of the Monasteries. Robert Hobbes, the abbot, was committed for trial for refusing to acknowledge the king's religious supremacy. Although a good and honest man he suffered the fate of all those who in that intolerant age committed 'treason'. He was hanged, it is said, together with the sub-prior and one of the monks, on an oak tree that still stands about two hundred yards from the south-west corner of the present house.

The first Russell of whom there is any record was Stephen Russell of Dorset, a merchant, probably a wine importer and MP for Wey-

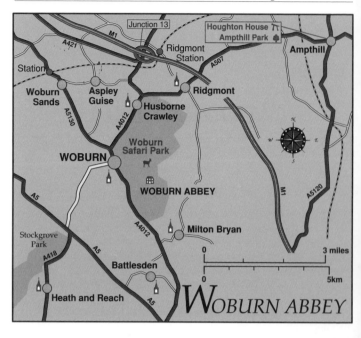

mouth in 1425, but the founder of the family fortunes was his great, great-grandson John Russell, who became the first Earl of Bedford. He was born about 1486 and at his death owned land or property in Devon, Cambridgeshire, London, Northamptonshire, Bedfordshire and Buckinghamshire. A Dorset country merchant, he served in the household of Henry VII for the last three years of the King's life. For the more valuable service he gave to Henry VIII he was created Baron Russell. After the King died in 1547 Russell was granted Woburn Abbey with land to the value of £100 a year. At the Coronation of Edward VI he was made Great Steward of England. He was created Earl of Bedford in 1550. The Covent Garden estate, valued at £50 a year, was acquired by Russell in 1552. It was sold just towards the end of World War I for £2 million.

John Russell never lived at Woburn — he may never even have seen it. He continued to live at Chenies, the inheritance of his wife. Nothing is heard of the abbey for the next 75 years except in 1572 when it was used to entertain Queen Elizabeth I on one of her periodic travels. The second Earl of Bedford asked Lord Burghley to ensure that the Queen stayed no longer than two nights and a day, presumably because of the expense.

Francis, the second Earl, was a godfather to Francis Drake and was the first Russell to adopt the family motto *Che Sara Sara* ,'What will be will be'. His grandson became the third Earl, whose wife Lucy acquired some of the older portraits in the house, including the Armada portrait of Queen Elizabeth.

In 1619 Francis, Lord Russell, acquired Woburn from his cousin, the third Earl, in exchange for a cash settlement. There is a fine portrait of Francis, the fourth Earl, by Van Dyck on the Grand Staircase. He was a patron of Inigo Jones, the designer and architect;

Woburn Abbey as seen from across the lake

together they built the Covent Garden piazza. It is possible that Jones may have acted as adviser in the partial rebuilding of Woburn for the fourth Earl. The north and south ranges of the monastic building were rebuilt; the family rooms, in Italian fashion, were in the north wing (the remains of the abbey church), and the State Rooms and the Gallery in the west wing. There were about ninety rooms in that early seventeenth-century house. The west range retained the buttressed front of the monastic original between projecting pavilions. That Jacobean north range survives today largely unaltered; the family lived there throughout the eighteenth century.

There was not much agricultural land attached to the house and the park was much smaller than it is today, extending to the north no further than the modern road that crosses it. When the park was eventually extended further north some of the fields at Husborne Crawley were swallowed up, and after 1760 about one-half of the village itself made way for the park extension.

William, the fifth Earl, lived through five reigns to the age of 87. He became the first Duke of Bedford and Marquess of Tavistock when William III in 1694 made amends for the execution of the Earl's son by Charles II for his part in the Rye House plot. William married Lady Anne Carr, whose fine portrait by Van Dyck is on the Grand Staircase.

The way of life in the Russell household is the subject of an absorbing book by Gladys Scott Thomson entitled *Life in a Noble Household 1641-1700*. In 1664, in the time of the fifth Earl (and first Duke) of Bedford, the total wages bill for the servants was £600 a year. The household staff included a receiver-general (salary £50 a year), a lawyer (who became a rich man from his commissions), a gentleman of the chamber, a steward, a chaplain, a bailiff, cooks, housekeepers, maids, footmen, porters, pages and watchmen. The household expenses included large sums for food, drink, fuel and luxuries. Coal from Newcastle and Scotland cost a ton.

Large numbers of oysters were eaten (at 1s 6d a quart). Wine was drunk in large quantities — accounts show that Bordeaux, Burgundy, port, sherry, brandy and champagne came in casks and bottles. Tea and coffee had recently arrived in England and was not yet popular. Tea was more expensive than coffee — Woburn paid between 23s and 3 guineas a pound for it. The fifth Earl was a heavy smoker — tobacco cost 2s 6d a pound (Virginian) or 9s a pound (Spanish) but pipes were cheap. The numerous portraits in the house cost money but in view of their value today seem inexpensive to us. Lely charged £25 to £30 for some portraits, and £60 for the Earl's portrait. Kneller charged £30 and £40 for two portraits in 1693-94.

Celia Fiennes visited the Jacobean house in 1697. It stood in 'a fine parke full of deer and wood'. She described the house as an old building, low, with very good stables and 'out offices'. The gardens were fine, with a large bowling-green, 'eight arbours kept cut neately', and a seat in a high tree that gave a view over the whole park. There were three large gardens full of fruit, which she described in some detail, obviously more taken with them than with the rambling old house. Daniel Defoe described the house as 'very ancient, spacious and convenient rather than fine, exceedingly pleasant by its situation', surrounded as it was by 'a great Quantity of Beach Woods and great Woods of Oak'.

The first Duke's grandson became the second Duke but he died at the age of 30. The third Duke was a spendthrift and if he also had not died early, at the age of 24 on a voyage to Lisbon, might have dissipated the entire family fortune. His grandmother-in-law was the redoubtable Sarah, Duchess of Marlborough, who held a low opinion of him.

John, the fourth Duke, was a man of an entirely different character. He held many high offices of State and saved the Woburn estate from bankruptcy. He was not happy with the house left by his predecessors; he wanted something much more ostentatious and was rich enough to afford it. He had interests in the West Country, in London and in shipping from all of which he derived his wealth. He created the dukedom and the Woburn estate of today. He devoted much time and money to filling the house with works of art and furniture; much of the French furniture was purchased by him in 1763 in Paris at the time when the fashion was changing from Rococo to neo-Classical.

He rebuilt Woburn in the mid-eighteenth century with the help of the architect Henry Flitcroft, transforming the Jacobean house into a Georgian palace but retaining the same area and even some of the rooms of the old house. The north and south ranges and part of the east range were retained but the west range was completely rebuilt. John Sanderson had drawn up the original plans in 1733 but it was Flitcroft who in 1747 began to rebuild the west range, the inner fronts of the other ranges and the two stable blocks. Among other improvements Flitcroft installed a hot-water bath and a water-closet.

The fourth Duke expanded the Woburn estate by purchasing when possible whole properties, the largest of which was the Ailesbury estate, which consisted of a large part of central Bedfordshire. Houghton House on the Ailesbury estate was partly demolished by the fifth Duke in 1794. During the eighteenth century the Russells bought about 200 large properties and many smaller ones

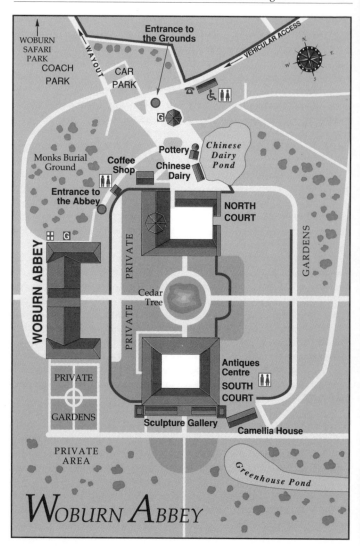

WOBURN SAFARI PARK

COACH PARK

CAR PARK

WAY OUT

Entrance to the Grounds

VEHICULAR ACCESS

N
E
W
S

G

Monks Burial Ground

Coffee Shop

Pottery

Chinese Dairy

Chinese Dairy Pond

Entrance to the Abbey

WOBURN ABBEY

G

PRIVATE

PRIVATE

PRIVATE

NORTH COURT

GARDENS

Cedar Tree

PRIVATE

GARDENS

Antiques Centre

SOUTH COURT

PRIVATE AREA

Sculpture Gallery

Camellia House

Greenhouse Pond

*W*OBURN *A*BBEY

including single cottages and small pieces of land. It was the fourth Duke who created the great park at Woburn. Acquisitions by Duchess Gertrude, his widow, continued after his death. She was his second wife and lived for 24 years after his death.

The common fields in twelve parishes on the Woburn estate were enclosed between 1796 and 1817, but Woburn village itself was not subjected to enclosure. The Woburn estate was again extended in 1842 by the purchase of the Ampthill estate from the Hollands and it reached its greatest extent in 1877, when it comprised 37,186 acres 58sq miles/150sq km, about one-tenth of Bedfordshire. The estate is now about 12,500 acres in extent.

Francis, the fifth Duke, gained some notoriety for taking a mistress in her fifties when he was only 21. He astonished everyone by becoming one of the most fluent speakers in the House of Lords. He also incurred the wrath of Edmund Burke when he presumed to criticise the amount of Burke's pension. After he tired of politics he became keenly interested in agriculture and was a member of the Board of Agriculture founding the annual sheep-shearing at Woburn.

He engaged the architect Henry Holland to make various modifications to the house, principally in the south wing, where the provision of elegant living-rooms enabled the family to move from the cold north wing that they had occupied for over 150 years. He also asked Holland to build a conservatory or greenhouse (now the Sculpture Gallery), a Chinese Dairy, a riding-school and a tennis-court. He died of a hernia at the age of 37 after a game of tennis.

After the fifth Duke the nineteenth-century Dukes were less in the public eye; they withdrew from office, remaining however politically active, and attended to the Woburn estate. John, the sixth Duke, was only one year younger than his brother, the fifth Duke. He was a keen farmer, a plant collector and a patron of the arts but he had extravagant tastes. He bought many pieces of classical sculpture in Rome during his travels in Italy, and later he rebuilt Covent Garden market in 1830.

The later Dukes added relatively little to the art collections. Francis, the seventh Duke, was a hard-working man, determined to rescue the finances of the estate from the excesses of the fifth and sixth Dukes, and during his 22 years as Duke he put the estate on a sound financial footing. His hospitality was well known — in one year alone 12,000 people were entertained, and that did not include the local people who waited outside the windows for the remains of the family meals. Two years after becoming Duke he entertained Queen Victoria and Prince Albert at Woburn for a few days, about a year after their marriage. He also bred racehorses, including three Derby winners, at his establishment at Exning, near Newmarket, which he purchased in 1845. No expense was spared to enlarge and equip the centre. Vice Admiral Rous who valued the stock after the Duke's death pronounced it 'the most perfect Riding Establishment.'

The eighth Duke was an invalid and had no children. The ninth Duke, his nephew Hastings, increased the family fortunes by renewing the leases of the Bloomsbury estates. He made large contributions to charity and good works and was generous to his tenants, but he died, cynical and embittered, in 1891. Sackville, the tenth Duke, enjoyed the dukedom for only 2 years.

Herbrand, the eleventh Duke, held the dukedom for 47 years. His wife was known as the 'Flying Duchess' and their common interest was animals. He was an extremely generous man and an enlightened landowner. The Duchess opened a cottage hospital at Woburn in 1898, and a military hospital at Woburn Abbey in 1914. This was later appointed one of the special surgical military hospitals, receiving convoys of wounded men direct from France.

Hastings, the twelfth Duke, was a strange man, whose activities during World War II embarrassed both his family and the Government. John, the present Duke, opened Woburn to the public in 1955 in order to raise money to preserve the house for posterity, a decision that has given pleasure to millions of visitors. It is now his eldest son Henry and his family who live there. Andrew, the present Duke's eldest grandson, is very involved in running the estate.

Woburn Abbey has evolved over a long period, from the time of the Cistercians to the rebuilding in the seventeenth and eighteenth centuries and its partial demolition in 1950. It is therefore less architecturally noteworthy than some other large country houses but what it lacks in that respect it makes up for in tradition and atmosphere. It is one of the stateliest of England's great homes. The seventeenth-century rebuilding has been attributed to Inigo Jones but as no building accounts survive it is not known who the architect was. The early Georgian rebuilding was by Henry Flitcroft, who was not an architect of the front rank but whose best work was done at Woburn, although his two stable blocks show more imagination than his somewhat derivative west wing. His only other major house was Wentworth Woodhouse in Yorkshire. The later Georgian additions (south range, east range and riding-stable), were by Henry Holland, a very capable architect.

The west front is still the same length as the medieval front; it even has the same number of windows. Flitcroft pulled down the west range and rebuilt it with the same number of rooms, but preserved the rooms in the two corner pavilions. The corner gables were replaced with Palladian attics and true Venetian windows replaced the former windows. The new range contained State Rooms on the first floor and a picture gallery on the courtyard front. The inner façade of the north range was refaced in the mid-eighteenth century and presents a Georgian front to the courtyard. The later inner façade of Holland's south range is plain. Nearly everything that is visible at Woburn therefore is eighteenth century, both inside and out, except the front of the north range and three rooms including the Grotto on the ground floor.

After World War II the east range was found to be infested with dry rot and in 1950 it was demolished together with about one-third of the north and south ranges. The east range, built by Holland in about 1787, was a long two-storey building, with a low portico and a cupola. The only consolation for its loss is that it was not particularly impressive and there is now a clear view of the inner court and the inner façade of the west range. Holland also built the riding-school and the tennis-court, which were demolished at the same time as the east range. The ends of the truncated north and south ranges were rebuilt in Classical style by Sir Albert Richardson.

The visitors' entrance is in the north wing, the oldest part of the building, which dates from the time of the fourth Earl in the early seventeenth century. Even when Flitcroft rebuilt the rest of the house this cold north wing continued as the family apartments until the fifth Duke decided to move to the south wing 50 years later. In the nineteenth century the **Book-Room** was the housekeeper's room and before that it was the fourth Duke's dressing-room. It houses an overflow of books from the Library, mainly on natural history, including a copy of Audubon's *Birds of America*. The hanging lamp was formerly lit by colza-oil obtained from local coleseeds, first cultivated near here in the early seventeenth century by refugees.

The tapestries in the **Fourth Duke's Bedroom** were woven at Mortlake between 1660 and 1664; the designs were based on Raphael's cartoons of the Acts of the Apostles, the originals of which are in the Victoria and Albert Museum. There is a portrait of Diana Spencer, favourite granddaughter of Sarah, Duchess of Marlborough. The ceiling of this room is decorated with four profile reliefs of the seasons.

The corridor known as **Paternoster Row** runs along the south side of the north wing; it replaced the north aisle of the abbey church. It contains cases of family mementoes and curios, such as the walking-stick given to the fifth Earl by Charles I in 1647. At the end of the corridor the Grand Staircase ascends to the first floor; each of its steps

The ornate Grand Staircase at Woburn Abbey

is held in place by the adjacent steps but the staircase appears to be quite safe. The family portraits include one by Lely and one by Van Dyck.

There are more portraits, mainly of the Dukes, in the Dukes' Corridor immediately above Paternoster Row. Woburn Abbey contains an extraordinary number of family portraits, probably the largest private collection in the country. From the first Earl onwards members of the family seem to have been obsessed by the desire to have their portraits painted. In 1700, when the first Duke died, there were 103 portraits in the Long Gallery alone. When Sarah Churchill came in 1732 she approved only of the portrait of Anne Carr.

The collection of portraits at Woburn illustrates the progress of painting in England from Tudor times to the nineteenth century, in particular in the late Tudor and early Jacobean periods. The nucleus of the collection was formed by Lucy Harrington, wife of the third Earl of Bedford, whose enthusiasm was mainly directed towards the paintings of Holbein.

The Chinese Room, a common feature of eighteenth-century stately homes

The eighteenth-century paintings by Reynolds and Gainsborough maintain the high standard set by those of Van Dyck and Lely of the seventeenth century. The fourth Duke and Duchess sat for Reynolds and Gainsborough several times. The Duke bought two of Gainsborough's early landscapes in 1755, but it was another 10 years before he commissioned portraits from him.

In the eighteenth century it was fashionable for stately homes to have a **Chinese Room**, and Woburn was no exception. Nearly all the furniture and ornaments in this room are Chinese. The wallpaper, which came from China in 1753, depicts a river landscape in great detail. The fourth Duke was a director of the East India Company, which traded with China. This room was once known as the Venetian room because of its window.

The eleventh Duke's wife was known as the 'Flying Duchess' because of her aerial exploits; the next room in the north wing, containing many of her personal possessions, is dedicated to her. Of her many interests animals, bird-watching and photography were prominent but she is best remembered for her record-breaking flights to India and South Africa. She was 61 when she made her first flight. Accompanied by an experienced pilot she flew to India and back in 8 days in 1929 and to the Cape and back in 17 days in 1930. Some of her journeys involved forced landings and considerable danger but her main worry was for the Duke should she not have survived. She disappeared one afternoon in March 1937 while attempting to complete 200 hours of solo flying. She had set off towards the Fens but ran into a snowstorm; pieces of the machine were found later on the East Anglian coast.

The **Yellow Drawing-Room** was redesigned in the 1760s for the fourth Duke. Most of the French furniture was purchased by him when he was Ambassador to France. He also redecorated the next room, now known as the **Racing Room** because of the numerous old and modern pictures of horses. The carpet in this room came from the 'Flying Duchess's' yacht *Sapphire II*. The Rococo ceiling is one of the best in the house.

At the north-west corner of the house are the State Rooms, which were kept mainly for the use of visiting Royalty. For the decorating and furnishing of the State Rooms the fourth Duke employed Samuel Norman, 'Cabinet-maker, Carver etc. of Soho Square'. In Queen Victoria's Bedroom there is a large painting by Hayter of Lord Russell's trial and underneath it some etchings by Queen Victoria and Prince Albert. The ceiling has a bold circular centre; its design was derived from Robert Wood's *The Ruins of Palmyra*, published in 1753. The State bed (dating from around 1740) was refurbished by

Samuel Norman with '39 yards best blue silk crepe fringe'. In Queen Victoria's Dressing-Room there are some fine Dutch and Flemish paintings, notably *The Valkhof at Nijmegen on the Waal* and *Fishermen on the Ice* (the River Maas) both by Cuyp.

In the three State reception rooms the decorations are of a luxurious mid-Georgian character but they must incorporate some earlier work because Norman charged for 'taking down and mending all the grand carved ornaments'. In each room there is a suite of gilt gesso chairs and settees. The elaborate mirrors between the windows are a feature of the State Rooms; they were made possibly by James Whittle, who had designed similar mirrors at Holkham Hall in Norfolk. Whittle carved the heraldic sculpture in the pediment of the west front.

In the **Blue Drawing-Room** (the blue of the walls has faded because of the sunlight) there are miniature replicas of some of the full-size paintings in the house, executed in 1853 in case of fire or other damage to the originals. In the nineteenth century afternoon tea was served in this room; Woburn was one of the first houses to adopt this practice.

The **State Saloon**, in the centre of the west wing and two floors in height, is in the same position and has the same area as the old saloon and is in the early Palladian style. The murals, painted in 1973 to replace the former blue silk damask, illustrate some of the places and buildings, such as Covent Garden, associated with various members of the family. The folio bookcase and tables may have been designed by Henry Holland. The fine chimney-pieces are by John Rysbrack (1756 and costing £195).

The ceiling frieze in the **State Dining-Room** was done by Flitcroft himself and the chimney-piece by Deval. The paintings include two Van Dycks and a Lely. The splendid Meissen dinner-service dating from about 1800 is decorated with birds and insects. As was usual in large Georgian houses the dining-room was situated a long way from the kitchen to prevent smells entering the house; food was kept warm by means of covers and burners. In the Reynolds Room there are nine pictures by the famous portrait painter.

The **Venetian Dining-Room** is in the south-west corner pavilion. It was remodelled by Holland to house the Venetian paintings by Canaletto that were in Bedford House in London until 1800. There are twenty-four paintings in all by the Venetian master; twenty-one in the room, another in the Blue Drawing-Room and two more on the top floor. It is thought that all these paintings were commissioned by the fourth Duke. From this room the different ground levels outside can be seen; the windows are at ground level on the south side and

State Dining-Room and table set with the splendid Meissen dinner-service

The Long Gallery

The Chinese Dairy in tranquil surroundings

The famous Armada portrait of Queen Elizabeth I

at first-floor level on the west side. The ground was built up along the south front by Holland to form a terrace above the brick vaults, to provide direct access from the new rooms to the garden.

Holland's south range contains the **Library** and its two ante-rooms. The Library is private but can be seen from the doorway. It is divided into three parts by pairs of Corinthian columns that support the upper floor. The stucco ceiling is different in style from those in the Flitcroft rooms. More portraits hang above the bookcases.

On the east side of the west wing parallel to the State Rooms is the **Long Gallery**, rebuilt between 1754 and 1756, which is also divided into three parts by pairs of columns; this room is one of Flitcroft's best pieces of work. When Horace Walpole saw it in 1751 it had seventeenth-century wood-panelling. The walls are lined with a Regency crimson paper and have curious panels with the Russell arms, a design sent to China to be painted on the Canton vases that stand on one of the mantelpieces. The most famous painting in the house is here — the Armada portrait of Queen Elizabeth I by George Gower.

In the vaults the porcelain display includes the Sèvres dinner-service presented to the fourth Duchess by King Louis XV of France to commemorate the signing of the Treaty of Paris in 1763. The service was for sixteen persons and although originally it consisted of 183 pieces not all of them have survived. All the pieces, except the tureens, are decorated with bouquets of flowers in white panels. Some of the pieces, such as the six-lobed tray and the wine-cooler, have unusual shapes. In this room there is also a model of HMS *Neptune* made by French prisoners in the Napoleonic Wars out of bones saved from their daily rations.

The **Silver and Gold Vaults** contain many interesting and beautiful pieces including a set of twelve silver-gilt teapots of 1803, but the greater part of the Woburn collection of silver dates from the eighteenth century. A group of pieces by Paul de Lamerie can be dated to 1737, the year of the fourth Duke's second marriage; it includes a pair of Rococo baskets and ladles and a set of six candlesticks. The Duchess's travelling-service in its mahogany case (1786) is by John Schofield. At the top of the stairs is the largest painting in the house, Murillo's *Cherubs Scattering Flowers*.

The **Grotto** is the oldest room in the house more or less in its original state, and dates from the early seventeenth century. Grottoes, like Chinese rooms, were once very fashionable; this one was originally open to the fresh air. Its stonework is carved to resemble seaweed and stalactites and its furniture to resemble sea-shells. Such an elaborate and well-preserved grotto is rare and it is probably the best example in England.

On the south side of the south stable block Holland constructed a conservatory, which was later converted to the **Sculpture Gallery**. It is not open to visitors as it is now a catering complex specialising in conferences, banquets and weddings. It has arched French windows and a central Venetian window under a pediment. Between 1801 and 1803 Holland added at one end of it an Ionic temple front, and in 1818 Wyatville added a new entrance and vestibules and a Temple of the Graces. The Camellia House forms a quadrant east of the Sculpture Gallery. In fact there was once a covered way from the house through the Sculpture Gallery to the Chinese Dairy, which enabled the family to walk in the dry to the fish-pond in inclement weather.

Holland's **Chinese Dairy** is polygonal, with a pagoda roof and a gallery along the side of the lake. In the park is the half-timbered Paris Exhibition House, built by Cubitt for the Exhibition of 1878; it is now a restaurant. In the south stable block is the Antiques Centre, consisting of fifty shops and show-cases owned by antique dealers in all parts of the country. One section on the ground floor contains four original shops first erected in London in 1780. The shops sell every imaginable type of antiques and bygones — furniture, glass, paintings, prints, silver clocks but no books.

Woburn Park and the **Safari Park** are perhaps the logical outcome of past ducal interests at Woburn — animals and agriculture. Animal conservation was one of the interests of the tenth and eleventh Dukes. The latter was President of the Zoological Society for many years, and deserves high praise for having saved the Père David deer from probable extinction. They had been hunted by Chinese emperors in their Royal parks and the only ones surviving after the Boxer Rebellion were a few that had been brought to Paris by the monk Père David. The Duke introduced six of them to Woburn and they began to breed; today there are about 600 Père David deer in the park. There is something uniquely beautiful about the sight of one of these herds grazing under English oak trees in the autumn. There are eight other species of deer in the park.

The Safari Park is a more commercialised aspect of these conservation interests. Animals here include zebra, rhinoceros, eland, hippopotamus, elephant, lion, tiger, timber wolf, giraffe, camel, monkey, black bear and bongo. Needless to say visitors must stay inside their vehicles while watching the animals. The fact that the animals appear to take little interest in people or their cars should not give visitors a false sense of security. The park security staff are never far away.

Père David deer in Woburn Park, the largest breeding herd in the world

✳ Woburn

Woburn is a perfectly-preserved (one could almost say fossilised) eighteenth-century village or small town. In the High Street and Bedford Street, which together form the main thoroughfare, there are many elegant red-brick Georgian houses, most of them rebuilt after a disastrous fire in 1724. The Market House at the main crossroads was built in 1830 by the architect Edward Blore to replace the former corn-market. He also added the upper parts to the tower of the medieval church, which is all that now remains of it. Adjoining the tower is the chapel of 1868, now redundant, which contains a monument of 1630 to Sir Francis Staunton and his family. Facing the tower is the old grammar school (1582), partly Elizabethan, partly restored by Blore, which by the eighteenth century had become an ordinary charity school.

The old church was once a chapel of ease to the parish church at Birchmore. It was replaced by St Mary's Church in Park Street, built by Henry Clutton for the eighth Duke of Bedford and consecrated in 1868. It is a very large and solidly-built church, and no expense was spared in its construction. Clutton used the late twelfth-century French Gothic style, seen to best advantage in the interior. He was a highly original architect not afraid of boldness in his churches, and

Woburn represents one of his best achievements.

There have been several disastrous fires in Woburn's history. In 1595 130 houses were destroyed and in 1645 a fire started by Royalist troops burnt about 18 houses. A third large fire in 1724 destroyed 39 houses. The old fire-engine house in High Street stands near the old grammar school. Woburn also suffered from the plague; 50 people died between 1625 and 1626 and 40 died in 1665. The fire in 1724 occurred just before Daniel Defoe wrote about the town and Woburn Abbey in his book *A Tour Thro' the Whole Island of Great Britain*. He said that as the town belonged to a noble family 'eminent for being good Landlords bountiful and munificent to their poor Tenants' there was no doubt that the town would be rebuilt, as it soon was.

In the countryside around Woburn there are one or two villages with interesting churches and a few miles away is the Georgian market town of Ampthill. The church of St Peter at **Battlesden**, 3 miles (5km) south of Woburn, stands in the park of a long-demolished Victorian country house. The house had been rebuilt and the park laid out by Joseph Paxton, the architect of the Crystal Palace in London. The church is quite remote, in a peaceful spot at the end of a lane, the only sound the wind in the surrounding trees. In 1846 the church was 'forlorn and neglected'. It dates from about 1280 and has a thirteenth-century chancel arch and a fifteenth-century tower. It is sparsely furnished but fortunately it escaped Victorian restoration.

The perfectly-preserved eighteenth-century village of Woburn

Segenhoe church, ½ mile (1km) mile south-east of Ridgmont village, ruined and ivy-covered, stands near Segenhoe Manor, the only surviving house of the medieval village that was once here. The church has an eleventh-century chancel and a re-set Norman south doorway. All the other village churches in the area are usually locked except those at Aspley Guise and Aspley Heath. The latter is another of Clutton's bold and imaginative designs, the same date as his church at Woburn (1868).

In the villages around Woburn it is easy to spot the houses built for the Bedford estate workers; they display a capital 'B', a coronet and a date of building. It should also be noticed how they increase in size from the mid-nineteenth century onwards. These plain semi-detached houses can be seen over much of the central and western parts of the county.

❊ Ampthill

The old market town of Ampthill stands on a hill, which meant that in the days of coaches it was not a popular stopping-place. The houses are therefore late rather than early Georgian; the early eighteenth-century White Hart Hotel is prominent. Church Street is Ampthill's most attractive street; Avenue House, the best house, was the home of Sir Albert Richardson, the architect who remodelled Woburn Abbey after the 1950 demolitions. The curious obelisk pump near the 1852 Moot Hall in the centre of the town was designed by Sir William Chambers in 1784; on it there are engraved distances to various destinations.

The remains of Houghton House stand one mile north of the town off the B530. This was the house partly demolished by the fifth Duke of Bedford in 1794 (he removed the roof and left the house to decay). It had been purchased by the fourth Duke in 1738. A mysterious building, it dates from the early seventeenth century, when it was owned by the Countess of Pembroke.

The obelisk known as Katherine's Cross in Ampthill Park commemorates Catherine of Aragon, who stayed at the house there while she was waiting for the verdict on her divorce from King Henry VIII. The obelisk became famous a few years ago as a result of the best-selling book *Masquerade* by Kit Williams. The illustrations in the book gave clues to the whereabouts of a model hare made of gold (worth £30,000) buried somewhere in England. It was in fact buried a few feet from the base of Katherine's Cross. Many people spent many months searching for the hare until one lucky person solved the riddles and found it.

Additional Information

Places to Visit

Woburn Abbey and Park
☎ (0525) 290350
Abbey Open: April to October, Monday to Saturday 11am-5pm. Sunday 11am-5.30pm. January to March, Saturday, Sunday 11am-4pm.
Park Open: April to October, Monday to Saturday 10am-4.45pm. Sunday 10am-5.45pm. January to March, Saturday, Sunday 10.30am-3.45pm. Coffee shop, gift shops, antiques centre, pottery, gardens and camping centre ☎ (0525) 290666
Directions: On M1 leave at junction 13: then A4012 to Woburn.
From A5 take A4012 to Woburn.
By rail, Bletchley (Intercity) is the nearest British Rail station.
Entrance to abbey and park from Woburn village.
Entrance to Safari Park from Woburn village or from A507 at Ridgmont. Reduced admission prices for senior citizens, students, children and handicapped persons in groups. Rooms available for dinner dances, conferences and weddings. Guided tours on request. Special programme for schools.

Antiques Centre
Open: daily, Easter to October 10am-6pm. November to Easter 11am-5pm. ☎ (0525) 290350

Woburn Safari Park
Open: March to October daily 10am-5pm. ☎ (0525) 290407
Restaurant, amusements, gift shop, picnic areas, boating lake. No dogs.

Tourist Information Centres

Woburn
Heritage Centre
Old St Mary's Church

Bedford Street, Beds MK17 9QB
Open: summer only.

Milton Keynes
Milton Keynes Food Centre
411 Seklow Gate East
Milton Keynes MK9 3NE
☎ (0908) 232525

Ampthill
12 Dunstable Street
Beds, MK45 2JU
☎ 0525 402051/406464

Accommodation and Eating Out

HOTELS
Woburn
The Bedford Arms Hotel
George Street ☎ (0525) 290441

The Bell Inn ☎ (0525) 290280

Aspley Guise
Moore Place
The Square ☎ (0908) 282000

Milton Keynes
Forte Crest
500 Saxon Gate West ☎ (0908) 667722

GUEST HOUSES
Woburn
Serendib
High Street ☎ (0525) 290464

Mrs Tough
11 George Street ☎ (0525) 290405

RESTAURANTS
Woburn
Paris House
Woburn Park ☎ (0525) 290692

The Bell Inn ☎ (0525) 290280

The Bedford Arms Hotel
George Street ☎ (0525) 290441

The Black Horse
Bedford Street ☎ (0525) 290210

4

BLENHEIM PALACE

When King Henry I decided to build a manor-house at Woodstock the landscape looked very different from that of today. There was neither lake nor bridge nor park and the River Glyme flowed past the site of the house in a steep-sided valley. At about the same time Henry created a deer-park, enclosed by a stone wall over 8 miles (13km) long, and stocked it with wild beasts. It was the predecessor of the present Blenheim Park and it may have been the first park in England with a stone wall surrounding it. When King Henry II inherited Woodstock Manor he founded the town of New Woodstock on waste ground outside the park gate to accommodate some of the Royal household and his guests when they came on hunting visits. The old village of Woodstock already existed half a mile to the north of the manor-house.

For the next 500 years Royalty continued to visit Woodstock Manor; the future Queen Elizabeth I was an involuntary guest, imprisoned there by her sister Mary in 1554-5. The garrison of the house surrendered to the Parliamentarians in 1646 but it was not destroyed, because it is said Cromwell's commissioners were driven out by a poltergeist. It was restored to the Crown in 1660. Sarah Churchill in 1709 finally ordered its demolition and a small memorial now marks its site on a mound near the northern end of the bridge and on its eastern side. The plinth of the memorial was designed by Sir William Chambers. In 1705, when the story of Blenheim Palace begins, the manor-house was in ruins and the park neglected.

When John Churchill, first Duke of Marlborough, returned to England in triumph after his defeat of the French at the village of *Blindheim* (Blenheim) in 1704, Queen Anne looked for some suitable gift to present to him 'from a grateful nation' and thought of

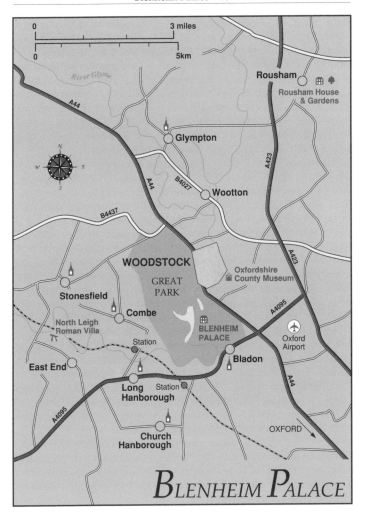

Woodstock Manor and its park. The royal bill transferring the manor to Marlborough was passed on 14 March 1705 and the Queen ordered the Board of Works to erect at her expense a house, soon to be known as the 'Castle of Blenheim'. No written agreement seems to have been drawn up, and this omission was the cause of endless recriminations and lawsuits in later years.

Sir Christopher Wren was invited to inspect the site and make a report; he gave an estimate of £100,000 for building the house, just one-third of the eventual cost of Blenheim Palace. The architect appointed to design and build the house was John Vanbrugh, the famous playwright, who held the post of Comptroller at the Board of Works but was an architect of limited experience. In 1700 Vanbrugh had begun the construction of Castle Howard in Yorkshire, which when completed proved that he was an architect of rare genius, although how much of the design of Castle Howard or of Blenheim Palace can be attributed to him and how much to his assistant Nicholas Hawksmoor will never be known.

Who exactly chose Vanbrugh remains a mystery, but Vanbrugh himself always maintained that Marlborough chose him in preference to Wren. Perhaps it was as well he did because the genial but persuasive Vanbrugh, although ceaselessly at cross-purposes with Sarah Churchill, was never deflected from his vision of building a palace worthy of the great commander. If Blenheim had been built by Wren it would probably have been more utilitarian in design in face of Sarah's cost-cutting exercises. Vanbrugh's salary was £400 per annum plus £200 'riding expenses', Hawksmoor's £300.

Blenheim is not so much a castle or a palace but more of a monument. Marlborough and Vanbrugh were in complete agreement that Blenheim Palace should be a memorial to Marlborough's achievements rather than a personal tribute to Marlborough, and in this aim Vanbrugh succeeded beyond all expectations. Only the Triumphal Arch and the Column of Victory, both added by Sarah Churchill, stand as memorials to Marlborough's personal glory.

Vanbrugh was asked to build a house similar to but larger than Castle Howard and to emphasise its monumental status. The principal difference between the two lies in the wings, which at Blenheim were brought forward to form two long arms. Most of the main apartments, corridors and stairs are in the same position as at Castle Howard. On the north side the Hall leads to the Saloon, the central room of a range of State apartments on the south side. Vaulted corridors connect the Hall with the private rooms in the east wing and the Gallery in the west wing.

The foundation stone of the palace was laid on 18 June 1705 — it is under the bow window on the east front. During the long years of Blenheim's construction Vanbrugh faced interminable troubles with lack of money, arguments with authorities, unsuitable stone, rain and frost, and not least with Sarah Churchill's implacable animosity and interference. Vanbrugh, however, was good-natured and optimistic otherwise he would assuredly have given up in despair before the building had progressed very far.

The orientation of the house was determined by the position of Bladon church tower. The south front is at right angles to a line joining the church tower and the centre of the house. The stone for the building came at first from local quarries but eventually from far and wide; in bringing stone from the Burford and Taynton quarries alone 136 carters were employed. When some of the local stone cracked after frost stone was brought from as far away as Portland and Plymouth. The chief masons were Edward Strong and his son, who had worked on St Paul's Cathedral. Twenty-two statues and most of the stone ornaments were executed by the famous carver Grinling Gibbons.

Vanbrugh engaged Henry Wise, gardener to King William III and Queen Anne, to lay out the gardens and landscape the park. In 1708 they were almost complete but in 1710 men were still working on the Great Parterre south of the house. Beyond the Parterre was the 'Woodwork', a hexagon-shaped wood interleaved with paths, and beyond that the walled kitchen garden, described by Vanbrugh as the finest in England. The walled garden survives today, the rest having been swept away by 'Capability' Brown later in the century.

The Grand Bridge was more like a mansion than a bridge for it had thirty-three rooms, their purpose always a mystery. It also contained an engine for pumping a continuous supply of water from Rosamond's Well to the living quarters in the palace. The Grand Bridge has always been greatly admired as an integral part of the landscape.

From the very beginning the supply of money from the Treasury was irregular and in 1712 it ceased altogether when the Queen lost interest in Blenheim and the Marlboroughs fell out of favour with her. Through the summers of 1706 and 1707 building continued; there were never fewer than 1,000 workmen employed at any one time. The Marlboroughs stayed in High Lodge on the west side of the park when they visited Blenheim. While the house was under construction and part of it already 27ft (8m) high it was decided to redesign the south front, increasing its height by one-third, involving the pulling down of two 60ft (18m) lengths. Whether the decision was Vanbrugh's or Marlborough's is not clear. Vanbrugh also took the opportunity to change the style of the north front from Doric to Corinthian.

To say that Sarah Churchill was unpopular would be an understatement. She was haughty, intolerant, bad-tempered, distrusting and parsimonious — yet she could be charming and nobody doubted her integrity. She ordered the old manor-house to be pulled down whereas Vanbrugh wanted to keep it as a romantic ruin — he

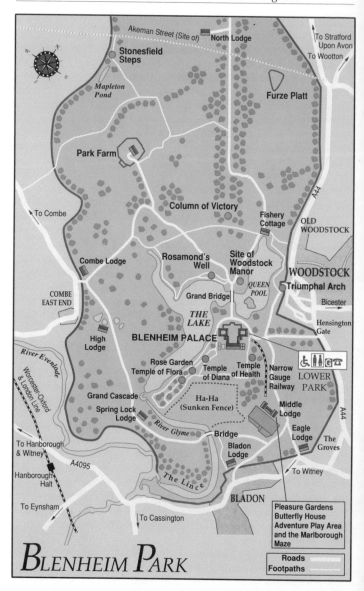

BLENHEIM PARK

Akeman Street (Site of)
North Lodge
To Stratford Upon Avon
To Wootton
Stonesfield Steps
Mapleton Pond
Furze Platt
Park Farm
Column of Victory
To Combe
Fishery Cottage
OLD WOODSTOCK
Combe Lodge
Rosamond's Well
Site of Woodstock Manor
WOODSTOCK
Triumphal Arch
COMBE EAST END
QUEEN POOL
Grand Bridge
Bicester
Hensington Gate
THE LAKE
BLENHEIM PALACE
High Lodge
River Evenlode
Worcester-Oxford & London Line
Rose Garden
Temple of Flora
Temple of Diana
Temple of Health
Narrow Gauge Railway
LOWER PARK
Grand Cascade
Spring Lock Lodge
Ha-Ha (Sunken Fence)
River Glyme
Middle Lodge
Eagle Lodge
The Groves
To Hanborough & Witney
A4095
Bridge
Bladon Lodge
Hanborough Halt
To Eynsham
The Lince
To Witney
To Cassington
BLADON

Pleasure Gardens
Butterfly House
Adventure Play Area
and the Marlborough
Maze

| Roads | |
| Footpaths | |

Blenheim Palace south front

Enjoying a game of cricket on the south lawn

was a romantic long before the Romantic movement became popular. So he ignored her orders and while the Marlboroughs were absent used some of the Blenheim money to make it habitable and lived in it himself for a while. When Sarah found out she was incensed and treated Vanbrugh badly, so much so that in 1716 he could stand no more and left Blenheim for ever.

In the spring of 1710 Sarah Churchill and the Queen fell out and never spoke to each other again. The Queen dismissed Godolphin, the Lord Treasurer, and Sarah ordered all work on Blenheim to cease immediately until more money was forthcoming. With Robert Harley as the new Lord Treasurer that seemed unlikely. The labourers at Blenheim had not been paid for a long time. Travers, the Surveyor-General at Blenheim, was so upset that he paid them £300 out of his own pocket. Harley allowed the Treasury to pay out £7,000, not to keep the labourers from starving but to prevent Marlborough from returning to England and stirring up trouble.

In June 1711 Vanbrugh's estimate for finishing the palace was £87,000; the Treasury had paid out only £30,000 of this by August. In December Marlborough was dismissed from all his posts as a result of a trumped-up charge. From June 1712 work slowly ground to a halt and most of the labourers and craftsmen left, Vanbrugh's verdict on Blenheim was that it was 'a monument of ingratitude'.

The money dried up completely and an air of calm descended on deserted Blenheim but in 1714 things changed dramatically. Queen Anne died, King George I ascended the throne, Marlborough was reinstated and Vanbrugh was knighted. Perhaps now Blenheim would be finished. It never was — the west court was not completed.

The Duke offered to pay for the palace to be finished (£60,000 out of a total cost of £300,000) but only if the Government settled all the outstanding debts first. The Government compromised — all men owed over £10 were given one-third of what was due to them and all owed under £10 were paid in full. In 1716 work recommenced but in the November Vanbrugh left for good having come to the end of his patience with the Duchess. Hawksmoor, Wise, Gibbons and the Strongs had also left; perhaps one of them could have been dispensed with but not all of them at once.

At this juncture hardly a single room in the house was finished. A visitor described it as 'chaos — only God Almighty could finish it'. It must have been tempting to leave it unfinished but the Marlboroughs were determined to complete it, even at their own expense. James Moore, a cabinet-maker, was placed in charge from 1717 to 1724. What he lacked in architectural knowledge, and he had very little, he picked up as he went along.

The Marlboroughs moved into the house in 1719, 14 years after its foundation and 8 years after Vanbrugh had first spoken about moving the furniture in. Building proceeded slowly. In June 1722 when the Duke died there was 10 years work still to be done. In his will he left £2 million — £50,000 of it for the completion of the palace. He had enjoyed only two summers of rest in his house and it had provided him with precious little pleasure in his lifetime, but it was after all built primarily as a monument and it will stand for ever as a tribute to his achievements.

Sarah Churchill became the richest woman in England. In spite of this she showed little concern for the debts owing to the workmen — in fact she sued 400 of them for money. She had £10,000 a year to spend on Blenheim ('to spoil it her own way' said Vanbrugh). But she neither spoiled it nor finished it. She completed the Gallery, the Chapel and the stables tower and there she stopped. After the house was completed Sarah was seldom there. On a surreptitious visit (he was banned from Blenheim) Vanbrugh observed that it was being finished 'in no good or graceful manner'. On another visit in 1725 he was refused admission — only Sarah could have been so petty.

For a long time after Sarah died nothing much was done to the house and park until George, the fourth Duke, employed Sir William Chambers to construct a new bridge over the river and the Temple of Diana, where Winston Churchill proposed to his future wife. The Duke found that he could not improve on Vanbrugh's work. In the fourth Duke's time about 187 rooms in the house were furnished.

Formal gardens were now out of fashion, however, and parks had to look natural and romantic, so the Duke called on Lancelot 'Capability' Brown, the country's foremost landscape architect, to 'improve' the park and gardens. Brown demolished the Great Parterre and grassed over the Great Court. To offset these lapses a stroke of genius created one of the most beautiful park landscapes in England. He removed the two causeways, except for what is now known as Queen Elizabeth's Island, and built a dam and a cascade on the river downstream of the bridge. A lake was thus formed on each side of the bridge, and the bridge itself was flooded to a depth of 15ft (4m). The height of the bridge is now much less than Vanbrugh intended, especially as the superstructure with which he intended to crown it was vetoed by the Duchess.

Brown worked at Blenheim from 1764 to 1774, replanting the whole park with belts and clumps of trees in his characteristic fashion, and rebuilt High Lodge with crenellations. King George III commented after viewing the park 'We have nothing to equal this' (on the royal estates).

The Grand Bridge

Sir Winston Churchill's Birthroom

Colourful autumn creepers on the Great Court pillars

Springtime in Blenheim Park

The ninth Duke employed Achille Duchêne to restore the Great Court, which Brown had grassed over, and to construct the Italian Garden in 1908 and the water terraces between 1925 and 1930. In 1950 Blenheim Palace was opened to the public (at half a crown or 12½ p) and they have been visiting in their millions ever since. Blenheim Palace is more than a monument, more than a museum, more than a house. It is a unique building, designed by two of the greatest of English architects, Vanbrugh and Hawksmoor, to commemorate the achievements of a general who never lost a battle.

Public access to the palace is through the east gate and the east court. The massive east gate, perhaps more than any other part of the palace, suggests the military origin of Blenheim, but there was a practical reason for its size. The top contained the cistern that held the water pumped from Rosamond's Well. The stone urns (and perhaps the statues) were carved by Grinling Gibbons. The inscription on the gate records the sum of money (£240,000) granted for the building of Blenheim by 'a munificent sovereign'.

The covered passages for the servants in the east court displeased the Duchess — she considered them extravagant. The kitchen in the south-west corner was deliberately sited a long way from the Dining-Room so that the smell of cooking could not permeate the house — a more important consideration than hot food. The orangery in the south-east corner was used as a theatre for the last time in 1789.

It is worth while pausing in the **Great Court** before entering the palace to study the north front in all its awesome majesty. Blenheim Palace represents one of the finest achievements of English Baroque architecture, of which Vanbrugh was one of the greatest exponents.

The roof-line of Blenheim is one of its chief glories. The choosing and the placing of the ornaments on the roof was a long business but the result is supremely successful. Vanbrugh was responsible for the overall effect but Hawksmoor probably designed most of the individual ornaments, including the 30ft (9m) finials on the square towers, as some of them resemble his designs for London churches; he called them his 'eminencies'.

Visitors enter the palace directly into the **Great Hall**. Its great height (67ft/20m) and its proscenium arch and columns are impressive but the overall effect is somewhat austere, typical of Vanbrugh. The decoration of the fluted Corinthian columns and the mouldings of the cornice are by Grinling Gibbons. Behind the arch is the former minstrels' gallery that was once open to the Saloon. The superb ceiling was painted by Sir James Thornhill; it depicts Marlborough kneeling before Britannia offering her a plan of the battle of Blenheim. For this he was paid £987, and for the murals 25 shillings a yard, far too much in the Duchess's opinion, so Laguerre was commissioned to paint the ceiling and walls of the Saloon.

By an odd quirk of fate Blenheim Palace is associated with two of the most famous Englishmen in history. The house was built for John Churchill, first Duke of Marlborough, and Sir Winston Churchill of more recent memory was born in one of the rooms west of the Great Hall. It is simply furnished, as it was at the time of his birth, in contrast with the other rooms in the palace. His mother Jennie, wife of Lord Randolph Churchill, was with a shooting party that weekend and was brought to this small room for the birth. Personal mementoes in the room include curls of Winston's hair, his baby vest and his wartime siren suit. In a nearby corridor there is a photographic montage of his life, accompanied by recordings of his wartime speeches.

In the corridor near Winston's Birthroom hangs a painting by Closterman of the first Duke and Duchess and their family and one by Kneller of the Duke on horseback. Here also there is a large collection of nineteenth-century lead soldiers representing those who fought under Napoleon.

Before reaching the Saloon visitors pass through the three rooms on the east side of it, the two **Drawing-Rooms** and the **Writing-Room**. The ceilings in all three rooms were designed by Hawksmoor, but the scrolls and eagles in the coving are much later (around 1890). The marble fireplaces date from the 1770s, and all the rooms are luxuriously furnished. The paintings in the Green Drawing-Room include two Knellers (both of Duchess Sarah), a Romney (the fourth Duke) and a Reynolds (Caroline the fourth Duchess). The beautiful clock mounted on a black bull was made by Gosselin of Paris. In the Red Drawing-Room the paintings include a Sargent (the ninth Duke and his family), three by Van Dyck (including Lady Morton and Mrs Killigrew) and a Reynolds (the fourth Duke and his family). It was the fourth Duke who engaged 'Capability' Brown to landscape the park; towards the end of his life he became a recluse and even refused to meet Lord Nelson when he called.

In the **Green Writing-Room** hangs the best known of all the tapestries in the house, which depicts Marlborough accepting the French surrender at Blenheim. The amount of detail in the picture is astonishing — burning water-mills, French troops crowding the village and the Danube in the distance. A painting of the third Duchess hangs over the fireplace.

The **Saloon** was formerly the State Dining-Room and is normally used by the family at Christmas. The ceiling and murals were undertaken by Louis Laguerre after Thornhill had completed his

The Blenheim tapestry

The Long Library at Blenheim Palace

*The majestic
Column of Victory*

*Blenheim Palace
east front*

own designs for them. Laguerre was cheaper than Thornhill (he charged £500) but one wonders what the latter would have made of the opportunity. Laguerre based his designs on the Escalier des Ambassadeurs at Versailles. The murals represent a colonnade open to the sky from which figures from the four continents look down. The caricatures include Laguerre himself and Dean Jones, Marlborough's chaplain. The white marble doorcases were designed by Hawksmoor; their arched heads are surmounted by shells and lintels resting on triglyphs, a favourite Hawksmoor detail; one of the doorcases was carved by Grinling Gibbons. The painting on the ceiling represents the Apotheosis of the Duke of Marlborough.

After the Saloon visitors pass through the three State Rooms on the west side. In all three rooms hang tapestries commemorating Marlborough's campaigns, commissioned by the Duke himself of the designer de Hondt and the Brussels weaver, Judocus de Vos. In the **First State Room** perhaps the most interesting tapestry is the one showing Marlborough about to attack the hilltop fortress of the Schellenberg, with the walled city of Donauworth in the distance. The other tapestries depict the battle of Malplaquet, the lines of Brabant and the siege of Lille. An interesting historical memento in this room is the letter that Marlborough scribbled on the back of a tavern bill immediately after the Battle of Blenheim and dispatched with all haste to the Queen and Sarah.

In the **Second State Room** a painting of Marlborough's adversary, Louis XIV himself, hangs above the chimney-piece, but the tapestries on either side of him remind us that he was defeated by the Duke. The **Third State Room** is magnificently furnished. Kneller's portrait of Marlborough shows him with Colonel Armstrong and a plan of Bouchain. Armstrong later built the waterworks in Blenheim Park. The large tapestry depicts the Battle of Oudenarde (1708). The gilded woodwork in these three rooms was commissioned by the ninth Duke in the 1890s and executed by a team of craftsmen from France.

The **Long Library** or Gallery was one of the last rooms in the palace to be completed. The decorations were designed by Hawksmoor, who probably also designed the marble doorcase. Hawksmoor considered the Gallery the most important room in the house; it was certainly his greatest achievement. The more one sees of Blenheim the more one realises that Hawksmoor had a hand in most things; throughout the whole palace, inside and out, there is hardly a single detail, other than paintings and murals, that with any certainty cannot be attributed to him. He divided the Gallery into five sections of unequal width and height, and lined the walls with giant Doric pilasters and a triglyph frieze.

The **Gallery** is 183ft (56m) long and was intended by Vanbrugh to be a picture gallery; it once housed the famous Sunderland library of 18,000 books assembled in the early eighteenth century. In 1882 the books were sold at auction by order of the seventh Duke for the ridiculous sum of £30,000, so instead of being donated to the British Museum they were dispersed among private collectors. The present library was collected by the ninth Duke. The organ of 1891 now at the north end of the room formerly stood in the central bay. The statue of Queen Anne and the bust of the Duke of Marlborough were executed by Rysbrack by order of Duchess Sarah.

The building of the **Chapel** was supervised by Hawksmoor and completed in 1732. Its orientation is curious, the altar being at the west end. The furnishings — reredos, pulpit, organ, benches, staircase — are Victorian. Dominating everything is the monumental tomb of the first Duke, designed by William Kent and carved by Rysbrack. It has larger than life-sized figures of the Duke and Duchess in classical dress with their two sons, and allegorical figures representing Fame and History. The Duchess chose the subject for the relief on the base — the surrender of Marshal Tallard at Blenheim. The Duke was first buried in Westminster Abbey but was reburied here when the Duchess died in 1744. The Randolph Churchill memorial (1895) has a figure in a shell niche with a surround of coloured marble.

The private apartments tour is an optional extra if they are not being used by the family. Included in the tour are the present Duke and Duchess's sitting-room and bedroom and the Bow Window Room, Sarah Churchill's favourite room, the only one where she felt at ease. She had explicitly asked Vanbrugh to provide a comfortable sitting-room for her own use. In this room the four Corinthian columns are by Gibbons, who also carved the marble fireplace.

Outside the palace the beautiful water-terraces were constructed between 1925 and 1930 by the ninth Duke out of a jungle of Victorian shrubbery and were the result of much thought and planning on the part of the Duke and his French architect Achille Duchêne. Their construction presented considerable problems but the result speaks for itself. The Bernini fountain is a scale model of the River-Gods fountain in the Piazza Navona in Rome. The features of the lead sphinxes are those of the ninth Duke's second wife.

The **Italian Garden** on the east side of the house, also created by the ninth Duke and Duchêne, can be seen from the south terrace. A formal garden consisting of a series of patterned beds, with Waldo Story's Mermaid Fountain at its centre, it is reminiscent of similar gardens at French chateaux. The ninth Duke also replanted the Great

The Marlborough Maze aerial view

Avenue with 4,000 yards of elms and repaved the Great Court.

The site of the Column of Victory, at the south end of the Great Avenue, was chosen by Sarah Churchill, although the Duke had favoured an obelisk on the site of Woodstock Manor. She rejected the designs of Hawksmoor and commissioned Lord Herbert to complete the monument. When it was finished she swallowed her pride for once and in desperation invited Lord Bolingbroke, once her bitter enemy, to write the inscription, and was so moved by his words that tears came to her eyes. It was described by Winston Churchill as 'a masterpiece of compact and majestic statement' and as the author of many such himself he was an authority. The other three sides of the base are inscribed with details relating to the estate and its inheritance. The column is 134ft (41m) high and is surmounted by a lead statue of the Duke of Marlborough.

The **Grand Bridge**, a major feat of engineering, was built to Vanbrugh's design by Bartholomew Peisley, the mason in charge. The main arch, 101ft (31m) wide, was finished in 1710. After its completion Sarah Churchill ordered the construction of a canal passing under the bridge and forming a pool to the west of it. This canal survived until Lancelot Brown dammed the river at Bladon, which flooded the valley and formed a lake on either side of the bridge. The result was undeniably more attractive than a single lake. The Grand Cascade was constructed by Brown at the west end of the lake. The bridge had been intended as the state approach to the palace but was never used as such because most visitors came direct from Woodstock.

The **High Lodge** on the west side of the park is the oldest of Blenheim's lodges. Since the crenellations were added in the fourth Duke's time it has had the appearance of a toy castle. Rosamond's Well is the oldest relic at Blenheim and perhaps the most romantic, with its legends dating back to King Henry II and his lover Rosamond Clifford.

Henry Wise's garden was on the south side of the house with many fully-grown trees being transplanted in its making, some of them still standing. The Parterre was rectangular and patterned with dwarf box. The 'Parterre' and the 'Woodwork' were enclosed by stone curtain walls with bastions, protecting them from the weather. The walled kitchen garden, still surviving, was also enclosed by a wall and set at an angle to the state gardens. Many varieties of peach, plum and pear were grown there, also figs, mulberries and quinces.

Some 600yd (550m) from the palace, and accessible by train, on foot or by car, the Pleasure Gardens include the Marlborough Maze, Butterfly House, Garden Cafeteria, Adventure Play Area, children's inflatable castle, putting greens, giant chess and draughts, and garden shop. The Pleasure Gardens, Marlborough Maze and Butter-fly House are open daily, 10am-6pm mid-March to the end of October.

Woodstock

❋

The long history of the town of Woodstock cannot be divorced from that of Woodstock Manor and Blenheim Palace, for it owes its very existence to the royal use of the manor. The town was founded by King Henry II to accommodate his guests; today it is a thriving centre owing some at least of its prosperity to thousands of people who visit Blenheim every year. Land was the key to wealth in the Middle Ages and Woodstock remained poor because it was confined to its original 40 acres. In 1279 it had 108 householders and about 540 inhabitants. The year 1453 was an important date for Europe and also for Woodstock for it received its first charter of incorporation as a borough. This was confirmed in 1558 and a new charter was forth-coming in 1664. In 1886 Woodstock became a municipal borough.

Two popular stories relating to Woodstock in the Middle Ages are without foundation. The first concerns Edward the Black Prince, who was allegedly born in a house in Old Woodstock; in fact he was almost certainly born in 1330 at Woodstock Manor, which was then the resort of royalty. The second story, which relates that Geoffrey Chaucer the poet was born at Woodstock, may have arisen because a house in Park Street has been called Chaucer's House for hundreds of years. A house on the site belonged to Thomas Chaucer, at one time Speaker of the House of Commons, who was probably the son of Geoffrey Chaucer.

Visitors should not miss the Oxfordshire County Museum in Park Street, which occupies Fletcher's House, an attractive town house with an eighteenth-century front. Its rooms relate the history of Woodstock and surrounding parts of the county from prehistoric to modern times, with an emphasis on local industries such as glove-making. Outside the museum are the town stocks, which have five holes. Opposite the museum is the parish church of St Mary Magdalene, which was once only a chapel of ease to the mother church at Bladon. The medieval church was largely rebuilt in 1878, but the tower is earlier (1785). The Bear Hotel is the most interesting of the many inns in the town. It consists of three quite different parts, a grand five-bayed Georgian block with a carriageway, a lower part of about 1700 with carved bears in the doorway, and a small six-teenth-century gabled wing.

At the far end of Park Street, beyond where it widens out to form a sort of courtyard, stands the Triumphal Arch through which visitors get their first astonishing view of Blenheim Palace and its park. The arch, designed by Hawksmoor in 1723, is a rather restrained piece of architecture not typical of his work. It was to have been set up where the Hensington gate now stands but a gardener refused to sell his cottage to the Marlboroughs to make way for it, to Sarah Churchill's intense annoyance. The site was finally purchased in 1773 and the Hensington gate was moved there from where it stood east of the house.

✳ Bladon

The village of Bladon, named after the River Bladon (the old name for the Evenlode), has a long history. In the early Middle Ages it was noted for its quarries, which supplied stone for Oxford buildings. Glove-making, as in Woodstock, has been a local industry for centuries. The village school was founded in 1858 by the seventh Duchess of Marlborough, and school treats and parties were always held at the palace. Bladon has recently become famous for its church, in particular for the graves in the churchyard. Although the church dates back to the eleventh or twelfth century much of the present fabric is no older than the restoration of 1891 and is of little architectural interest. It was formerly the parish church of Woodstock as well as of Bladon, when the church at Woodstock was only a chapel of ease.

The tenth Duke and Duchess were the first Marlboroughs to be buried here; their graves are by the wall on the east side of the churchyard. Lord Randolph Churchill, father of Winston, was buried here in 1895 and his wife in 1921. Sir Winston Churchill died on 24 January 1965, 70 years to the very day after his father died, and buried in a simple grave. The funeral was private, unlike the state funeral at St Paul's Cathedral, which was attended by statesmen from all over the world. Lady Churchill was buried with him on her death in 1977. Other graves include those of Consuelo Vanderbilt Balsan (ninth Duchess, 1965); Winston's children Diana (1963), Randolph (1968) and Sarah (1982), Winston's brother John (1947), and Christopher Soames (1987), husband of Mary, Winston's other daughter.

♣ Rousham

Rousham Park, a few miles north of Woodstock, is a place of pilgrimage for students of the Romantic movement in English landscape history and in particular the work of William Kent, who revolutionised garden design in England. Rousham was part of the first phase of English Romantic landscape design and remains much as Kent planned it, one of the few gardens of this date to survive unscathed. Kent was engaged by the owner, General James Dormer, in 1738. He planted new trees to obscure the straight avenues then existing, and placed temples and ornaments in strategic positions. North of the house is the bowling green and beyond it a steep slope with a wide view of the countryside. The house, originally built in 1635, was remodelled by Kent in 1738. He added two side wings and a stable block and after his transformation the house resembled an early Tudor palace. The south entrance front is virtually as he left it, except for the replacement of the glazed windows. Much of the interior of the house is the original sixteenth-century work. Rousham is not commercialised and is delightfully unspoilt.

Oxford

It is impossible here to detail all the places and buildings in Oxford that might interest visitors. For a start there are twelve museums in the city, ranging from the Ashmolean, the oldest public museum in the country (founded 1683), to the Telecom Museum, one of the newest. The thirty-four Oxford colleges can be visited during the vacations and at certain times during term. The cathedral (entrance from Tom Quad at Christ Church College) is open every day; its spire is one of the earliest in England. The rather scanty remains of the castle are in New Road, most of its site now occupied by the County Hall and prison. Needless to say in a university city there are many excellent bookshops both new and secondhand, including Blackwell's, one of the largest in the world. Full information on all these places and many more is obtainable from the Tourist Information Centre in St Aldates. From here there are official sightseeing tours of the city on foot or by bus. Car-parking is difficult in Oxford and visitors are advised not to drive into the city but to take advantage of the park-and-ride facilities on the outskirts.

Additional Information

Places to Visit

Blenheim Palace

Open daily 10.30am-5.30pm (last admission 4.45pm) mid-March to 31 October.

Gift shops, Pleasure Gardens, restaurant, cafés, coaches welcome. Inclusive ticket: Palace Tour, Church-ill Exhibition, Park, Garden, Motor Launch, Train, Butterfly House, Adventure Play Area, Nature Trail and Parking.

Optional: The Marlborough Maze and Rowing Boat Hire.

Directions: M40 from London: leave at Junction 9. A40 to Oxford. A44 from Oxford or Evesham. A4095 from Witney or Bicester. By rail, Oxford (Intercity) is the nearest British Rail station ☎ (0865) 722333. Scheduled bus services run from Oxford (Corn-market St) to Woodstock, stopping at the Park Gates (For details ☎ (0865) 727000 or (0865) 711312). Entrance to Blenheim Palace and Park at Woodstock on A44. ☎ (0993) 811325 24hr telephone recorded information service.

East End

North Leigh Roman Villa
Open: Good Friday or 1 April (whichever is earlier) to 30 September daily 10am-6pm.

Rousham

Rousham Park
Open: April to September
House: Wednesday, Sunday, Bank Holidays 2-4.30pm.
Gardens: daily 10am-4.30pm.
☎ (0869) 47110

Woodstock

Oxfordshire County Museum
Open: May to September, Monday to Friday 10am-5pm. Saturday 10am-6pm. Sunday 2-6pm. October to April, Tuesday to Friday 10am-4pm. Saturday 10am-5pm. Sunday 2-5pm. Café, gift shop.☎ (0993) 811456

Tourist Information Centres

Oxford
St Aldates
Oxford, OX1 1DY
☎ 0865 726871

Woodstock
Hensington Road
Woodstock
Oxfordshire, OX7 1JQ
☎ (0993) 811038

Accommodation and Eating Out

HOTELS

Woodstock
The Bear Hotel
Market Place ☎ (0993) 811511

The Feathers Hotel
Market Street ☎ (0993) 812291

The Marlborough Arms Hotel
Oxford Street ☎ (0993) 811227

The Kings Arms Hotel
Market Street ☎ (0993) 811412

Vickers Hotel
Market Place ☎ (0993) 811212

Oxford
List from Tourist Information Centre

RESTAURANTS

Woodstock
Brotherton's Brasserie
High Street ☎ (0993) 811114

Wheelers
Market Street ☎ (0993) 811412

5

WARWICK CASTLE

W arwick Castle is rightly described as the finest medieval castle in England. It is situated at Warwick, on the River Avon, some 20 miles (32km) south-east of Birmingham. The town has retained much of its medieval character too, despite a large fire in 1694. The old market town retains two of its gateways, with chapels above the archways and the Lord Leycester Hospital. It was established in 1571 by the Earl of Leicester as an old soldiers' home, near to the west gate. It includes a unique candlelit chapel, a galleried Courtyard, a Great Hall, Guildhall and other timber-framed buildings.

In an area steeped in history, Kenilworth Castle is nearby together with Shakespeare's Stratford-Upon-Avon 10 miles (16km) to the south-west. There is much to see in the area. It is referred to as England's historic heartland and central to this is Warwick Castle.

Here Kings and Queens of England were entertained. One of its owners — Richard Neville, Earl of Warwick was known as 'The Kingmaker'. He was sufficiently powerful to hold two kings in captivity at one time, including King Edward IV, whom he had created king and who was actually held as a prisoner here at Warwick; he even ruled the Kingdom for a while. It was owned also by Ambrose Dudley, the brother of Robert Dudley, Earl of Leicester and favourite of Queen Elizabeth I. The Queen stayed here while on her way to Kenilworth Castle, Robert Dudley's home. King Richard III started to improve the fortifications while living here in the fifteenth century.

Warwick Castle therefore occupies an important place in the history of England. Here history was moulded; people associated with it run like a thread down the centuries, close to the heart of the nation. The stirring history of Warwick Castle is well documented in the Castle guide book.

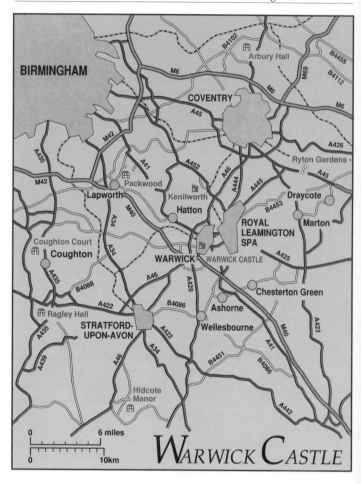

The Castle has the advantage of being largely complete. It does not enjoy the size of some of the Welsh castles of similar age, such as Conway (with its array of towers along huge walls surrounding the town as well as the castle itself) or Caernarvon. Yet with its massive Guy's and Caesar's Towers and its huge Gatehouse and Barbican, Warwick stands as a symbol of intrigue and power in medieval England, of influence in Tudor times and of affluence in the more settled later centuries.

The history of Warwick spans virtually 1,000 years. Today, visitors may enjoy the military aspects of the Castle. As an alternative, and in complete contrast the State Rooms are open to visitors and other rooms recreate a social gathering of leading aristocrats and Royalty in the closing years of the last century. Madame Tussaud's, the current owners, have brought their famous wax-works characters to Warwick and recreated a Royal weekend party in 1898. It is a huge success, making Warwick the most visited stately home in Britain.

One needs a full day here. In addition to the above there is also the Victorian Rose Garden, recreated from the original plans and now featuring a new pink-flowering English rose especially named 'Warwick Castle'. The original Norman motte survives with part of its thirteenth-century wall intact. Its original bailey or courtyard is still preserved in the line of the later fortifications. Beyond the motte are the grounds landscaped by Lancelot (Capability) Brown; in fact Warwick was his first independent commission. Here is the Conservatory, built in 1786 and now housing an exact replica of the Warwick Vase.

Warwick Castle and the River Avon

Part of the original medieval road bridge survives over the River Avon close to the Castle. A new footbridge below the castle allows access onto River Island which enables the vast extent of the river frontage to be seen, viewed from a suitable angle. Additionally, there is a river walk, Woodland Park as well as the Peacock Garden near the Conservatory to explore. Finally, if you are feeling fit, there are the walls to explore with Guy's Tower and Caesar's Tower to climb. It is all of 128ft to the top! The gardens are, by and large, suitable for wheelchairs but the buildings involve many steps.

Warwick Castle is easy to reach. The main road into town from the M40 passes the castle drive on the right close to the centre of town. The number of carparks is a ready indicator of the popularity of the Castle. Leaving the vehicle behind (assuming you arrive by car), a Plant Centre is passed on your left. It offers for sale many of the plants seen on the estate, so if you see something you particularly like, make a note of the name and enquire here if it is available. The 'Warwick Castle' rose may be bought here.

The first building you reach is the old stable block. There is a café here and a shop, both available before entering the admissions area. Once through there is a restaurant upstairs (The Stables). A further restaurant is in the Undercroft, situated below the State Rooms. There is also the Riverside Refreshment Kiosk near to the footbridge over the river and tables to sit at on the adjacent grassed area.

As one emerges from the Stable block, one cannot fail to be impressed by the grandeur of the Castle with Guy's Tower and a huge ditch surrounding the curtain wall. This was always a ditch and not a water-filled moat, being situated quite a height above the river. The pathway to the Castle leads past the entrance to the **Victorian** **Rose Garden**. The site had become overgrown and almost forgotten. It had been set out in 1868 to the design of an eminent landscape gardener, Robert Marnock. Fortunately, two plans survived which indicated what the garden had looked like, even down to details of the ironwork. The garden was recreated, including fresh ironwork to support new climbing roses.

During this restoration work an old rock garden was found adjacent to the Victorian Rose Garden. This was identified as being the rock garden on a plan of 1900 and was also refurbished. It also provides a good vantage point for the Victorian Rose Garden.

Within the latter are two ice houses which date from 1830. They are conical in shape and were used for storing ice for use in the house (for chilling wine and food etc). Ice would last for up to two years in these chambers. They have been restored and are open to view. A filling hatch in the roof lets in sufficient light to enable one to see the chamber once your eyes have adjusted to the subdued light.

The recreation of the Victorian Rose Garden was commemorated by the development of a new and beautiful pink rose. It is appropriately called 'Warwick Castle' and occupies the centre bed of the garden. Before deciding whether to investigate the gardens or the buildings first, have regard to the weather. If rain looks likely, it may be worthwhile exploring the gardens first before entering the Castle.

The Victorian Rose Garden is open all year and the peak flowering period for the garden is late June and through July. At this time, the garden is bedecked with flowers. The recreation has been a great success and the garden well worth visiting particularly at this time of year.

Circulating around the Victorian Rose Garden, one leaves it opposite the bridge over the Castle ditch. This brings one to the **Barbican** and Gatehouse, the heavily fortified entrance to the Castle. With its double portcullis and murder holes where boiling pitch etc could be poured on the unsuspecting attacker, it must have presented a formidable appearance in medieval times. The Castle was in fact twice attacked by Royalists during the Civil War, but the attackers gave up after only two weeks! Nonetheless this garrisoning of the Castle for Parliament saved it from destruction after King Charles I was beheaded. The Barbican formerly had a drawbridge on the site of the bridge.

The guide book is very useful for describing the Castle's military history. The adjacent town had been fortified in Saxon times, but after the Norman Conquest of England in 1066 the new King, William I, set about subjugating the north of England and built a chain of castles to protect his rear as he advanced northwards. One of these castles was here at Warwick. A mound of earth, or motte, was thrown up and a wooden stockade built upon the top. A large adjacent area, or bailey was surrounded by another wooden stockade which was eventually replaced with stone. This thirteenth-century stone wall survives in part to this day on the top of the motte which is known as Ethelflëda's Mound, after the daughter of Alfred the Great. She was the builder of the wall around the town.

On the bailey, protected by the surrounding wall, a hall would have been built together with other buildings, both domestic (such as a kitchen, bakehouse, chapel etc) and military (garrison buildings, armourer's shop, blacksmith and accommodation for servants). The hall was built on the river side of the courtyard and the rest on the north side up against the north wall, away from the hall. These buildings were later replaced by more substantial stone-built buildings. The hall had enormously thick walls, up to 9ft (3m) in width.

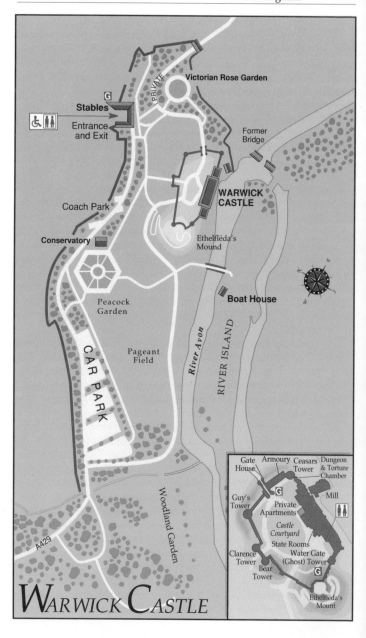

Victorian Rose Garden

PRIVATE

G Stables

Entrance and Exit

Former Bridge

Coach Park

WARWICK CASTLE

Ethelflëda's Mound

Conservatory

Boat House

N
E
W
S

Peacock Garden

Pageant Field

River Avon

RIVER ISLAND

CAR PARK

Woodland Garden

A429

Gate House
Armoury
Ceasars Tower
Dungeon & Torture Chamber

Guy's Tower

G

Mill

Private Apartments

Castle Courtyard

Clarence Tower

Bear Tower

State Rooms

Water Gate (Ghost) Tower

G

Ethelflëda's Mount

*W*ARWICK *C*ASTLE

Peacocks have been a feature of Warwick Castle grounds for a long time

An archway festooned with flowers in the Rose Garden

Although the principal domestic buildings became more affluent, especially after the end of the castle's military importance, they were, by and large, modelled within the ancient fortress.

Fortification of the Castle in a major development started in the fourteenth century. First Caesar's Tower was built around 1340 followed by the Gatehouse slightly later and Guy's Tower about 1395. Nearly a century later, the last Royal Keep in England to be built was started by Richard, Duke of Gloucester — later King Richard III. Richard spent some time here, but he survived as King for only 2 years before he was killed on Bosworth Field in 1485. It was never completed and of what was built, much was demolished so that only the northern two towers survive. Richard III was the son-in-law of Richard Neville, the 'Kingmaker'. The two rear towers were demolished in the early seventeenth century and would have considerably intruded into the Courtyard.

Access to the castle wall may be obtained at **Clarence Tower**. This is the right hand tower of the Royal Keep. It is named after Richard III's brother George, Duke of Clarence. From the tower steps it is possible to look into a gun room with three gun ports from which cannon would have protruded. This room would have given protection to the nearby Guy's Tower and fire could also have been directed into the ditch. There is also a doorway here (a Sallyport) from which soldiers could leave the protection of the tower to launch an attack of their own.

Emerging at the top of the Clarence Tower, the lowest of the Castle's towers, the castle wall gives access to **Guy's Tower**. It is 128ft (39m) high and much of the building work may have been earlier than the completion date, held to be 1395 or thereabouts. It is twelve-sided and five stories high, with two spiral staircases. One reaches from the top to the curtain wall, and the other from top to bottom. On the four lower floors there is a chamber, together with a sitting room (complete with fireplace) and one other room. The top floor has an hexagonal guardroom, similar to Caesar's Tower. A climb to the top of the tower affords a panoramic view over the castle and the town.

Climbing down, one can then walk along the wall to the Gate-house, and along a walkway over the clock mechanism. A further and final stretch of castle wall gives access to **Caesars Tower**. A short climb brings one up to the parapet, where those with a steady nerve can wander around the outside of the tower and enjoy the view. The main staircase can then be taken to return to ground level. At the parapet level of the tower is a guard room, similar to Guy's Tower and there are three storeys below, plus a dungeon at the base. This tower drops almost to the river and the total height of 147ft (45m)

makes it higher than Guy's Tower. Through the gaps in the projecting floor of the parapet (called 'machicolations') stones could be
dropped upon attackers below.

The various rooms of the tower have, like Guy's Tower, been used
in the past to house prisoners. French prisoners captured at the battle
of Poitiers are said to have been held here and other prisoners were
held here during the Civil War. They would have enjoyed considerably more comfort in these rooms relative to the **Dungeon**, where
inscriptions reveal that some people were held here for several years.
The Dungeon may be seen by taking the flight of steps from the
Courtyard down into the base of the tower.

Perhaps of more interest are the displays of instruments of torture
or the contents of the **Armoury**. Access to these displays may be
made from the Courtyard. The Armoury contains a knight on
horseback in full armour. Further armour may be seen in the Great
Hall in the State Rooms. One leaves the Armoury through the shop
to emerge into the Courtyard by the side of the Gatehouse.

A set of steps leads up to a suite of rooms in the Gatehouse at first
floor level. From the various doorways it is clear that the Gatehouse
and the Barbican contain quite a few rooms. Those open to visitors
are considered to have been quite a comfortable suite. It includes a
main living room and even a small closet/bedroom built into the
thickness of the external wall. There is a display here devoted to King
Richard III. It goes someway to dispel some of the early propaganda
spread about the King by his enemies. Before moving away from the
Gatehouse, there is a bookshop in one of the ground floor rooms.

The Courtyard now has a main central lawn and was raised
several feet in height by Capability Brown. This is noticeable as one
drops down towards the gateway through the wall between the
Castle mound and the Bear Tower.

There are two distinct sets of apartments to be visited — the State
Apartments and the smaller more comfortable rooms to the east end
of the building which houses the wax works tableau on the **'Royal
Weekend Party, 1898'.**

Guests at the party included two Royals, the Prince of Wales, later
King Edward VII, together with the Duke of York. Given the Prince
of Wales's reputation with unaccompanied ladies, one is left to
speculate whether the presence of Millicent, Duchess of Sutherland
is a subtle indication that she was his companion. She was the half
sister to the Countess, so all may have been quite above board!

As you enter the first room a butler welcomes guests. This room,
like the others which follow it, have all been restored to their 1898
appearance. Modern fittings, including lights, have been removed

Shining armour in the Great Hall

The Music Room, once the heart of social occasions

The Marquess of Blandford and his nurse, in the Royal Weekend Party tableau

and replaced by reproduction period pieces. The Castle had electricity at the time, although the Countess preferred gas and candle power, which was kinder to her complexion.

The next room is the **Library** where the Earl of Warwick is seen engaged in conversation with Sir Winston Churchill, the eighth Duke of Devonshire and Lord Brooke. It is perhaps not obvious how good a choice of characters was made in this grouping. The Duke was a very close friend of the Prince of Wales. After the Duke's marriage in 1892, his wife Louise (who had been his mistress for thirty years) hosted some of the finest social gatherings in the land, as well as many parties for the future King who could enjoy himself discreetly with his friends and mistresses at Chatsworth. The Warwick's were in that select group with the Duke and Duchess of Marlborough and their kinsman, Winston Churchill, who was born at Blenheim, the Marlborough's home. Here, the twentieth century's greatest Prime Minister talks to the Duke, a cabinet minister described as 'the best Prime Minister the nineteenth century never had'.

One cannot help seeing the model of the Duke here without thinking that this was the man described as being dressed like a 'seedy, shady sailor' and the comment he made quietly whilst listening to a Parliamentary debate in the House of Lords that 'the greatest moment of *my* life was when my pig won first prize at Skipton Fair!'

In the next room guests are being entertained by the singing of Miss Clara Butt, accompanied on the piano by Signor Paolo Tosti. Turning the sheets of music is the Earl's daughter, Lady Marjorie Greville. Listening are Mr George Cornwallis-West, Lady Randolph Churchill (Winston's mother) and, Louise, Duchess of Devonshire. She was known as the Double Duchess, having previously been married to the Duke of Manchester.

The next room shows the Duke of York, son of the Prince of Wales and the future King George V, playing cards with the Duke of Marlborough.

In yet another beautiful room, the Countess of Warwick may be seen taking tea with Millicent, Duchess of Sutherland. Climbing the staircase, one passes a bathroom where a maid can be seen running the bath. The Duchess of Marlborough, daughter of William Vanderbilt, is then seen preparing for her bath; a change of clothes lies ready for her.

Moving onto the landing, one passes a nurse carrying the infant Marquess of Blandford on your right and then a further room where the Earl's valet is filling a hip bath. A change of clothes lie ready on the bed.

The Dowager Countess sits in the next room, being attended by her maid. The dressing table mirror has been carefully positioned to give a reflection of her features, as she is seen sideways from the landing. In the next room, Mary Curzon is seen looking out into the Courtyard. She was the wife of George, Lord Curzon, the future Viceroy of India, who lived at the beautiful Robert Adam-built Kedleston Hall, near to Derby and now owned by the National Trust.

Field Marshall Lord Roberts VC is seen next, adjusting his tie. He was the hero of the Afghanistan expedition to relieve Kandahar and was shortly to leave for South Africa where he became Supreme Commander of British forces in South Africa. The bedroom furniture in this room is worth examining closely before proceeding to the next room where the Prince of Wales is seen talking to Lord Curzon. In order to get to the Prince of Wales's room one has to cross a passageway where four clerestory windows look down into the Great Hall. These had been blocked up, but after a fire on 3 December 1871, they were re-opened.

Most of the panelling in this bedroom is sixteenth century, although some is nineteenth. Some of the panelling you walk past conceals a wardrobe built into the walls. The sight of the Prince recalls to mind a story told against his close friend, the Duke of Devonshire, who was notorious for his untidy attire. On one occasion the Prince had to admonish his friend for wearing the Order of the Garter upside down. It was typical of the Duke that he had not noticed. It is equally possible that he did not even realise!

The Countess's bedroom is then seen with a maid making final adjustments to the Countess's gown before she goes to meet her guests. Here the tableau ends and a staircase leads down to the Courtyard. Tussaud's careful recreation of the wax models is a great success. It creates in a unique way an impression of Victorian life in a country house. The rooms come to life in a way that is most unusual. The comparison is all the more distinct as one wanders around the adjacent State Rooms.

Having reached the Courtyard, to the left down the stairs is the Undercroft, if refreshments are needed. Alternatively, round to the right is the entrance to the Chapel and the tour of the State Rooms.

The **Chapel** dates from the early seventeenth century, although it may be on the site of a much earlier chapel. It is fairly plain, compared for instance with Chatsworth or Castle Howard, but it does have one or two rather interesting features. Take a close look at the illuminated Italian vase. It is not too old, dating from about 1830, but exhibits some rather delicate carving. Another carving worth looking at is the wood carving of the Battle of the Amazons and dating from around

The Cedar Drawing Room

Madame Tussaud's wax models create a life-like impression of Victorian society (The Boudoir)

1740. Observe also the rather nice fan vaulting on the ceiling before passing the organ to reach a passage way which leads into the **Great Hall**.

This huge room lost its roof in the 1871 fire and a new hammerbeam roof had to be provided. You are within the massive walls of the fortified Great Hall of medieval times, as you can plainly tell if you look at the window recess. The Great Hall includes some fine armour. Much of it dates back to the sixteenth century. More unusual is a fourteenth-century cooking pot for the military, now known as 'Guy's Porridge Pot'. The huge oak Kenilworth buffet was made for the Great Exhibition of 1851. It shows scenes recalling Queen Elizabeth I's visit to Kenilworth Castle in 1575, where she

Sweeping lawns create the setting for this view of Warwick Castle

stayed as the guest of Robert Dudley.

The **State Dining Room** is one of the most beautiful rooms in the house. It is panelled from floor to ceiling and is dominated by an equestrian portrait of Charles I. It is from the studio of Sir Anthony van Dyck and there are another four known portraits very similar to this one. Facing this painting are two eighteenth-century paintings whose frames are a work of art in themselves. The paintings date from 1736 and 1737 and portray the Prince and Princess of Wales. The latter was Princess Augusta of Saxe-Gotha and she gave her name to the two cities in Georgia and Maine, USA. In this room the Prince of Wales and the other guests of the house parties would have dined. It must have looked splendid!

Returning to the Great Hall, the next room is the **Red Drawing Room**, one of several enfiladed rooms facing the river. These rooms were created in the late seventeenth century. The house guide book contains a good description of each room. In this room are some fine English School paintings, a Louis XV Boulle Bracket Clock and two Louis XV Boulle china cabinets with a Chinese service. Of particular interest are two chests which have painted panels dating from 1470 to 1480 and they are the oldest paintings in Warwick Castle.

The large **Cedar Drawing Room** comes next. It takes its name from the cedarwood panelling installed in 1670. It is finely carved and compliments the plaster ceiling executed by English craftsmen. With its eighteenth-century furniture and beautiful carrara marble fireplace, this room is a great achievement.

The **Green Drawing Room** follows and is a complete contrast. It is lighter, completely different in style and is full of small paintings. There are also four Japanese banqueting dishes of about 1690, held in much later giltwood tables. They surround a sixteenth-century Florentine table top inlaid with semi-precious stones. Apparently this was once a billiard room. The ceiling is coffered and adds considerable elegance. In fact every room in the house seems to have a differently designed ceiling!

The ceiling in the **Queen Anne Bedroom** which follows is definitely out of keeping with the four poster bed which now occupies the room. This was the Queen's bed from Windsor Castle. It was the gift of King George III to the Earl of Warwick and complete with its giltwood suite of furniture, also shown in this room. It faces a large full length portrait of the Queen, who ruled from 1702 to 1714. Hanging in this room are Delft Tapestries dating from 1604. They are magnificent and exceedingly detailed and are among the most important items in the collection.

The last of the State Rooms on the tour is the **Blue Boudoir**. This is a charming room, with some intricate wood carvings, both by local wood carvers and some attributed to Grinling Gibbons. There are a number of small portraits here, but the room is dominated by the portrait of King Henry VIII. With the surrounding wood carving it is complimented by a somewhat plainer fireplace below. There are lovely views down the river and over the park from here.

One returns along a landing with views down into the Courtyard. On display here within a glass case is Queen Elizabeth I's saddle, together with her handkerchief and Great Seal. The landing leads you back to a set of steps which leads down to the Undercroft Restaurant and the exit into the Courtyard once more.

On returning to the Courtyard, the **Watergate Tower** is on your left, so named because it gave access to the river. The suite of rooms in this tower were used by Sir Fulke Greville during his restoration of the Castle. He had acquired it from King James I in 1604. He had been Chancellor of the Exchequer to Queen Elizabeth I as well as her Treasurer of the Navy before that. He was later a Privy Councillor to King James I. He was murdered in 1628 by his servant, Ralph Haywood. Apparently his ghost is said to haunt the tower. There is a study as well as a bedroom. The former is panelled and a portrait of Greville hangs here. The bedroom, or bedchamber as it would have been known, has a seventeenth-century four poster bed. It creates a good idea of perhaps how the suite would have looked while Fulke Greville was restoring the Castle. There is also a good viewpoint across the Courtyard to Guy's Tower from here. There is a small shop at ground level as you leave the building.

This completes a tour of the Castle. However, there is still more to be seen with the hexagonal Peacock Garden and the Conservatory being the main feature beyond the Castle. The **Conservatory**, originally called the Greenhouse, was built to house the Warwick Vase. The current vase is in fact a copy, made by Plowden & Smith of London in 1991. It weighs half a ton and is made of polyester resin and marble dust. The original marble Warwick Vase, was dug up in pieces at Hadrians Villa near Tivoli in 1770 and is believed to date back to AD78. The vase's many admirers included the Emperor Napoleon Bonaparte of whom it was said: 'Had he been successful in conquering England, the first note in his pocket book was to possess himself of the marble vase at Warwick.'

It was acquired, however, by Sir William Hamilton, the British Envoy Extraordinary to the Court of Naples whose wife Emma Hamilton became Lord Nelson's mistress. Sir William described it as 'the finest vase in the world surely'. It is reputed to have cost £300 to have the vase reconstituted and repaired and it was offered to the

British Museum who declined it. The vase was then acquired by Sir William's nephew, the Earl of Warwick, although it is not known how it got to England or how much was paid for it.

The vase was originally placed in the Castle Courtyard but was later moved to the Conservatory, which was specially built to house it by William Eborall in 1786. The vase remained in the Conservatory for two centuries until it was acquired by Glasgow Museums and Art Galleries in 1978. It is now on display as part of the Burrell Collection. It has a diameter of nearly 6ft (2m) and holds 163 gallons. The Conservatory now houses a variety of warm climate plants. There is a pleasant view from here down to the river.

Below the Peacock Garden — there are quite a few peacocks, roaming freely, all completely at home with all the visitors — the Pageant Field stretches down to the river. There are specimen trees here, including two which were planted by Queen Victoria and Prince Albert. A riverside walk may be taken down the river to the Woodland Garden and Foxes Study. This area extends to the bend in the river. The river island may be reached by a bridge and from the bridge one can examine the massive river frontage of the Castle. Beyond the mill and the weir, the remains of the medieval bridge can still be seen. The central portion was washed away, shortly after the Earl built the new Banbury Road bridge. Fortunately for us quite a lot survives, either side of the missing section. This completes a memorable visit to an essential part of England's heritage.

Enjoy boating on the river in the spectacular surroundings of the castle

Additional Information

Places to Visit

Warwick

Warwick Castle
Open: all year except Christmas
Day. March to September: 10am-
5.30pm; October to February:
10am-4.30pm.
☎ (0926) 408000
Directions: Warwickshire is
situated 2 miles (3km) from the
M40. It is signposted on the
motorway at junction15. Follow
the signs towards Warwick and
Leamington Spa. Warwick and
Stratford are both served by rail.

Lord Leycester Hospital
High Street
☎ (0926) 491422
A fine medieval hospital, chapel and
guildhall. Incorporates the museum
of the Queen's Own Hussars.
Open: 10am-5.30pm summer,
closed Mondays. 10am-4.30pm
winter, closed Sundays.

Oken's House and Doll Museum
Castle Street
☎ (0926) 495546
One of the finest collections of
early dolls in the country displayed
in Oken's House.
Open: from May until end
September. Monday to Saturday
10am-5pm. Sunday 2-5pm.

Warwickshire Museum
Market Hall
Market Street
Enquiries ☎ (0926) 410410
Part of the county museum
collection housed in the eighteenth-
century Market Hall.
☎ (0926) 495546
Open: Monday to Saturday 10am-
5.30pm, Sunday (May to September only) 2.30-5.30pm.

Collegiate Church of St Mary
Old Square
Enquiries ☎ (0926) 400771
Famous for its Beauchamp Chapel,
Medieval/tudor tombs and tower.
Brass rubbing.
Open: winter 9am-4pm. Summer
9am-6pm.

St John's Museum
St John's
☎ (0926) 410410 ext 2021
A charming Jacobean mansion
housing period reconstructions of a
parlour, kitchen and Victorian
classroom. Also costumes, musical
instruments and Royal Warwick-
shire Regimental Museum.
Open: 10am-12.30pm, 1.30-5.30pm
(Tuesday to Saturday). Closed
Mondays. Sunday (May to
September only). Also Bank
Holiday Monday 2.30-5pm.

*Warwickshire Yeomanry Museum and
Warwick Town Museum*
The Cellars, Court House
Jury Street (entrance in Castle Street)
Enquiries ☎ (0926) 492212
Uniforms, arms, swords, sabres
and selected silver.
Open: most Fridays, Saturdays,
Sundays and Bank Holidays. Easter
to end of September 10am-1pm and
2-4pm.

Alcester
Ragley Hall
☎ (0789) 762090
Beautiful seventeenth-century
Palladian House, home of the
Marquess of Hertford. Park
contains adventure wood, maze,

children's amusements, country trail and sailing lake.
Open: Easter to end September every day except Monday and Friday. House: 12noon-5pm. Garden and Park 10am-6pm July and August. Garden and Park only open Monday and Friday 10am-6pm.

Coughton Court
☎ (0789) 762435
Mainly Elizabethan house, formerly moated, the wives of some of the Gunpowder Plotters awaited the results of the plot in the central gatehouse. Shop and Cream Teas.
Open: April, Saturday and Sunday 1.30-5.30pm and also 21-23 April. May to end September daily except Monday and Friday (Bank Holiday Mondays 1.30-5.30pm). October Saturday and Sunday also 27-29 October 1.30-5.30pm.

Arbury Hall
2 miles (3km) south-west of Nuneaton
☎ (0203) 382804
An Elizabethan Country House with beautiful plaster ceilings, pictures and fine specimens of period furniture.
Open: Sundays from Easter to end September, also Bank Holiday Mondays.
Hall: 2-5pm. Gardens 2-6pm.

Ashorne
Ashorne Hall
Near Warwick
☎ (0926) 651444
Brings to life the sounds, nostalgia and atmosphere of the mechanical music entertainment. Magnificent Compton Cinema Organ accompanying silent comedies in an authentic replica of a 1930's picture house.
Open: please telephone for times.

Banbury
Broughton Castle
☎ (0295) 262624
A moated castle, dating back to the fourteenth century.
Open: mid-May to mid-September, Sunday and Wednesday, also Thursdays in July and August (also Bank Holiday Sundays and Mondays including Easter) 2-5pm.

Upton House
☎ (0295) 87266
Late seventeenth-century house with collection of old master paintings, Brussels tapestries. Terraced garden and lake.
Open: April and October Saturday, Sunday and Bank Holiday Monday 2-6pm. May to end September, Saturday to Wednesday 2-6pm. May to end September, Saturday to Wednesday 2-6pm.

Charlecote
Charlecote Park
Near Wellesbourne
☎ (0789) 470277
The house, originally Elizabethan altered in the nineteenth century. Contains kitchens, brewery, carriages and tap room.
Open: April to end October daily except Monday and Thursday. Open Bank Holiday Mondays. 11am-6pm. House closed 1-2pm daily. Closed Good Friday.

Chesterton
Windmill
Off the Fosse Way, approx 5 miles (8km) from Warwick
☎ (0926) 412435
Early seventeenth-century stone windmill built in 1632.
Open: occasional open days usually in autumn. Can be inspected externally at any time.

Danchurch
Draycote Water County Park
☎ (0926) 493431 ext 2342
Views from hillside overlooking
Draycote Reservoir, waterside
picnicking and adventure playground. By Junction 1, M45, south-
west of Rugby.
Open: sunrise to sunset.

Farnborough
Farnborough Hall
Banbury
☎ (0295) 89593
Classical eighteenth-century house,
grounds contain temples, terrace
walks, also in Estate Yard, Edgehill
Battle Museum.
Open: House, Grounds and Terrace
Walk, April to end September
Wednesday and Saturday 2-6pm. 3
and 4 May 2-6pm. Terrace Walk
Thursday and Fridays 2-6pm.

Hatton
Hatton Country World
George's Farm
Hatton off A4177 or B4439
☎ (0926) 842436
Converted farm buildings now
housing craft workshops. Rare
breeds of farm animals.
Open: selection of workshops
daily, all year 10am-5pm.

Hidcote Bartrim
Hidcote Manor Garden
Nr Chipping Campden
Gloucestershire GL55 6LR
A series of small gardens within
the whole, separated by walls and
hedges of different species. A
famous garden now owned by the
National Trust. Licensed restau-
rant, plant centre, shop.
Open: April to end of October,
daily except Tuesday and Friday

(11am-7pm). Closed Good Friday.
Last admissions 6pm or 1 hour
before sunset if earlier.

Hockley Heath
Packwood House
☎ (0564) 782024
A timber-framed Tudor house with
mid-seventeenth-century addi-
tions. Collections tapestry,
needlework and furniture.
Open: April to end September,
Wednesday to Sunday and Bank
Holiday Mondays 2-6pm. October
Wednesday to Sunday 12.30-4pm.
Closed Good Friday.

Kenilworth
Kenilworth Castle
☎ (0926) 52078
Dramatic ruins of a great castle
fortress. Exhibition of Elizabeth I.
Open: Easter to October Monday to
Sunday 10am-6pm. October to Easter,
Tuesday to Sunday 10am-4pm.

Lapworth
Baddesley Clinton
☎ (0564) 783294
A moated medieval manor house
little changed since 1634.
Open: Beginning March to end
September, Wednesday to Sunday
(open Bank Holiday Monday)
12.30-6pm. October 12.30-4.30pm.
Closed Good Friday.
Restaurant and shop open Novem-
ber to mid-December as above.
Owned by the National Trust.

Leamington Spa
*Leamington Spa Art Gallery and
    Museum*
Avenue Road
☎ (0926) 426559
Paintings by Dutch and Flemish
masters. Twentieth-century
paintings and watercolours, mainly
English. Local history exhibits.

Open: all year Monday to Saturday
10am-1pm and 2-5pm. Thursday
evenings 6-8pm. Closed Sundays.

Jephson Gardens
☎ (0926) 311470
13 acres of beautifully laid out
gardens. Tropical bird house, wild
ducks use lake.
Open: daily all year 8am-sunset.

Marton
Marton Museum of Country Bygones
Louisa Ward Close
Marton ☎ (0926) 633361
Hand tools of craftsmen — thatch-
ing, wheelwrighting, saddlery, shep-
herding. Farm hand tools, household
and dairy equipment and wagons.
Open: Easter to October daily
10am-7pm.

Ryton-on-Dunsmore
Ryton Gardens
☎ (0203) 303517
Demonstrates gardens cultivated
naturally without the use of
pesticides and artificial fertilisers.
Speciality vegetables, fruit, herbs
and flowers.
Open: April to September daily 9am-
6pm. October to March 10am-4pm.

Stratford-Upon-Avon
Oxtall Stud Farm and Café
Warwick Road
☎ (0789) 205277
Stud Farm with café for cream teas,
also coaches welcome.
Open: Easter to end September.

Royal Shakespeare Theatre
Stratford-Upon-Avon
☎ (0789) 295623

Wellesbourne
Mill Farm
Kineton Road
Wellesbourne, Warks CV35 9HG
☎ (0789) 470237

Wellesbourne Watermill
Working watermill, grinding flour.
Nature trails, cream teas in eighteenth-century timber-framed barn.
Open: Easter to end September
11am-4.30pm (Thursday to Sunday
only). Rest of year: 2-4pm (Sunday
afternoons only).

Tourist Information Centre

Warwick
The Court House
Jury Street, Warwick
☎ (0926) 492212

Accommodation and Eating Out

Warwick
Warwick Castle
Medieval banquets are held on
Friday and Saturday nights in the
Undercroft, throughout the year.
Advance booking may be advisable
on ☎ 0926 495421.
Warwick Arms Hotel
17 High Street
Warwick CV34 4AT
☎ (0926) 492759
300-year-old coaching inn.

Lord Leycester Hotel
Jury Street
Warwick CV34 4EJ
☎ (0926) 491481
Georgian hotel in centre of town.

Hilton National
Warwick (at junction 15, M40)
Stratford Road
Warwick CV34 6RE
☎ (0926) 499555
Luxury hotel with swimming room
and fitness centre.

Forth House
44 High Street
Warwick CV34 4AX
☎ (0926) 401512
Small, inexpensive hotel.

6

CHATSWORTH

To the east of Bakewell in Derbyshire the River Derwent flows south through a wide and pronounced valley. Heather-clad moorlands to the east of the valley give way to coppices and grassland. The former road between Bakewell and Chesterfield crossed the river at Edensor. Here a manor house existed by the river, the home of the Leche family through eleven generations. The estate was purchased in 1549 by Sir William Cavendish and his wife, Elizabeth — Bess of Hardwick as she is more popularly known. This house had been sold to John Agard by Francis Leche, who had married Bess's sister. When Agard died, William Cavendish bought it back into the fold for £600.

Bess built a large house, to the south of the old house. It was four and five stories in height and built around a courtyard. The house guide book has an excellent artist's impression of it in September 1699 when the south front had been re-built to its current design. Bess's house was battlemented, with towers and lots of chimneys. In the middle of the west front was an in-built gatehouse with V-shaped towers on either side. These were five storeys high and a large archway gave entry to the house.

William Cavendish was the gaoler of Mary, Queen of Scots and she was held under house arrest at Chatsworth on six occasions — 1569, 1570, 1573, 1577 and between 1578 and 1579 . It is traditionally held that the moated feature close to the bridge over the River Derwent was where the ill-fated Queen took fresh air. It is known as Queen Mary's Bower to this day.

Today very little remains of the Elizabethan house, it was replaced during a relatively short period of time with the main house as we now see it. It stands four-square against the hillside; a continuing and opulent reminder of the strength and wealth of the family that built it. An extensive north wing was added in the nineteenth century which fortunately survived a threat of demolition earlier this century. The house was set against a magnificent park landscaped by 'Capability' Brown. It was he who had planted the various woodlands which today look so natural a part of the landscape. Chatsworth was Derbyshire's first house of national importance. It was to be followed by Kedleston near Derby later in the eighteenth century. However Chatsworth was furnished without regard to expense. The Cavendish family was running a vertically integrated industrial empire as long ago as the seventeenth century. It is not without good reason that Bess of Hardwick has been regarded as being as wealthy and as potentially powerful as Queen Elizabeth herself. Investment in the arts over four centuries kept Chatsworth's collection in a position of national importance.

Bess's great grandson was created the first Duke of Devonshire by a grateful King William III following his successful contention of the throne. The first Duke commenced the redevelopment of Bess's house by demolishing the south side and building the current south front. The work, which was started by William Talman in April 1687, was to transform the house over generations into both a home and a vast treasure house, both in terms of its decorations and its collection. In *The Derbyshire Country House* by Craven & Stanley, which described the County's main country houses, the description of Chatsworth ends thus: '… this unique and important house and its environment. It has few, if any, rivals in the British Isles'. However its development was staggered over two centuries combining the best craftsmanship available, in terms of painting and carving, both in stone and wood.

The redevelopment, because of its piecemeal fashion meant that certain aspects of the original house became embodied in the fabric of the new. Bess's house was characterised by having its State Rooms on the top floor of the south front and here they remain. The Great Hall became the current Painted Hall. The east front of the original house is believed to have been similar to the west front with the angle towers at each corner. The north-east and south-east towers, containing circular stair wells remain. They were accommodated within the design of the east front by narrow projections close to the ends of the front. These were highlighted by Wyattville in the nineteenth century who added giant pilasters to them.

Talman's work on the south front was a great success, although his external horseshoe-shaped staircase down to the garden was removed and replaced by the current one in 1837 by Wyatville. The front was broken up by the narrow projecting angle pavilions with their Ionic pilasters. The carving on the frieze of Cavendish knots and the carved stags antlers on the key stones over the upper windows occur only on these pavilions, which gives them a greater emphasis. The central portion of the front is comparatively plain but the whole is united by the cornice which supports the balustrade with its urns.

The redevelopment of the south front was followed by the great staircase which was in the east range opposite the main entrance — as may still be seen at nearby Hardwick Hall, also built by Bess of Hardwick. The great staircase went off the Great Hall and in between 1689 and 1691, the latter was also replaced by the Painted Hall. So much of the east front had been removed, that the whole front was re-designed by Talman. This was completed in 1696, whereupon Talman was dismissed by the Duke after a disagreement. The front is rather plain, and because of rising ground the basement story is hidden from view.

This set the scene for a mystery which may never be resolved. In 1700, the construction of the west front began. It took three years to complete but the designer is unknown. Possibly it bears some influence by Talman and even John Vanbrugh, who was soon to start work at Castle Howard, could have been involved. He stayed at Chatsworth for four to five days in 1699. Vanbrugh was also involved later at Blenheim Palace.

The west front was a great success. It is imposing without being overpowering, its height creating an impression of compactness which is actually deceiving. The pilasters built by Talman into the angle pavilion of the south front were continued on the west front. However instead of the comparatively plain central section of the south front, the centre of the west front has attached columns supporting a pediment above. This was carved by Samuel Watson. He was a man of exceptional talent and equally happy working in both wood and stone. So fine is the quality of much of his wood carving in the house that it was for a long time attributed to Grinling Gibbons. Despite his undisputed skill he remained essentially a local man throughout his career. The frieze was continued together with the balustrade above it. Either side of the two central windows were carved garlands by Henri Nadauld, who also moved on to Castle Howard. The ground level had dropped sufficiently to allow it to be a ground floor and the main entrance was incorporated here, despite it being somewhat insignificant in its proportions.

The piecemeal development continued with the construction of a colonnade and gallery over on the courtyard side of the south front. However, the final stage of the reconstruction was to follow shortly afterwards. In 1705, the north front was built, taking two years to

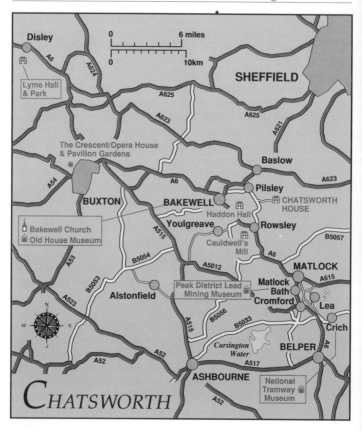

complete. Consequently over a period of twenty years the house was completely transformed in appearance. Despite the work having been executed in such a piecemeal and complicated manner, it presents the appearance of a unified whole. The continuity of the frieze, balustrade and urns and pilasters contributed to this, but the short building period clearly was also influential.

However the development of the north front was not without its problems. There was a 9ft (3m) difference in the lengths of the west and east fronts! This was overcome by the construction of the large bow of five bays divided by huge Corinthian pilasters. It is worth recalling that Chatsworth was the earliest house outside London to be furnished with sash windows.

The historic Chatsworth House lies in some of the Peak District's most picturesque countryside, West Front (above) and South Front (below)

In the nineteenth century, additional alterations were made to the structure by Sir Jeffry Wyatville, on behalf of the sixth Duke. His first work was the conversion of the long gallery into the library in 1815. However in 1820, the construction of the north wing began. It is 357ft (109m) long and contained the dining room, sculpture-gallery, orangery, banqueting room, pavilion, kitchens, servants quarters, theatre etc. It was intended that the old State Rooms would become 'a museum of old furniture and a walk in bad weather' according to the sixth Duke's handbook.

Clearly the success of the external elevations would be matched by work on the interior. The first Duke employed the best artists of the time to decorate his imposing seat. These included Antonio Verrio, Louis Laguerre and his father-in-law, Jean Tijou, the French ironsmith, Caius Gabriel Cibber, Samuel Watson, who carved the west front pediment, his son Henry Watson and many more, including several other local craftsmen.

The house is approached down an avenue of tulip trees. On the left are rooms in Wyatville's extension. By the front door is a fine weeping ash tree. It was brought here in 1830 when it was already forty years old, from a garden in Mile-Ash, near Derby. A local firm specialised in the removal of mature trees and there is a feature on this at Elvaston Castle near Derby, where several trees were moved. To reach the house, the gates and posts had to be removed at the south lodge in order to get the tree through!

One enters the house into the **North Entrance Hall**, where you can buy the house guide book. This room was the former kitchen and steps lead up to a corridor leading to the Painted Hall (to the left) and private rooms (to the right). In the corner of the room is a Roman carving of a mother and child. The sixth Duke followed the fashion for collecting statuary in the early years of the nineteenth century and this is one of many that he collected to be seen both inside and outside the house.

Proceeding via the North corridor, one approaches the **Painted Hall**. The corridors around the courtyard were originally open colonnades which gave access to the Painted Hall for visitors using the main entrance on the west front. The Painted Hall is huge (60ft/18m in length, 27ft/8m) in width and like the chapel, rising the height of two stories. The ceiling and upper wall paintings are original and were painted by Laguerre. The ground floor has seen several alterations however. The floor was replaced by Henry Watson as long ago as 1779, but the sixth Duke changed the design and had it relaid. The room originally had two curved staircases rising to the entrance to the Great Staircase. This was demolished by the sixth Duke who put in a straight flight and galleries on both sides of the room. In 1912 the stairs and the galleries were removed and replaced by the current stairs and the single gallery on the west side.

The Great Stairs lead up to the State Rooms on the second floor. At the bottom, and in view from the Painted Hall, is a bronze statue of Mercury, cast for the sixth Duke. The casings of the doorways are particularly well carved in Derbyshire alabaster. Off the top of the stairs are the **Scots Rooms** together with the **Wellington** and **Leicester Rooms**. These were built by the sixth Duke to make additional bedrooms and have been refurbished by the present Duke and Duchess. A tour of these rooms — the only bedrooms open save the State Bedroom — is an optional extra for which an additional minimal charge is made. The name 'Scots Rooms' is a relic of the days when Mary, Queen of Scots stayed here. Even if the Queen stayed in a room in this part of the house, the furnishings are of a later date, along with the rooms.

The Scots and Leicester Rooms are small and cosy and a complete contrast to the State Rooms. The first and largest is the **State Dining Room**. It has a notorious ceiling painted by Verrio and Laguerre which shows 'The Fury' cutting the thread of life or fate with her shears. In actual fact it shows the portrait of the first Duke's housekeeper whom Verrio disliked. This is a sumptuous room enriched not only by the two painters, but also by the truly magnificent carvings. Some are by Samuel Watson, but much in this room was carved by London craftsmen. The carvings adorn the overmantle, adjacent limewood panels and other features in the room. The Dining Room and the other State Rooms were enfiladed and a large mirror placed at the end in order to give the appearance that the passage was much longer than it actually was.

During World War II, the house was used by the girls of Penrhos College, having been evacuated from Colwyn Bay after their buildings were commandeered by the Ministry of Food. The State Rooms soon had their quota of beds. In *School Days at Chatsworth*, one has a fascinating insight of the great house in use as a school. The State Drawing Room housed 21 beds; the Music Room 15 beds and the State Bedroom another 16. There were even another 16 in the south gallery, laid end to end! Dustless chalk and pencils were the rule and only the sixth form could use ink. Chemistry was banished to the Stables! Edward Halliday painted the State Drawing Room in use as a dormitory and this may be seen in that room today. It is the next room to the State Dining Room.

The walls of the **Drawing Room** are hung with Mortlake tapestries and date from about 1635. They are after Raphael's cartoons which

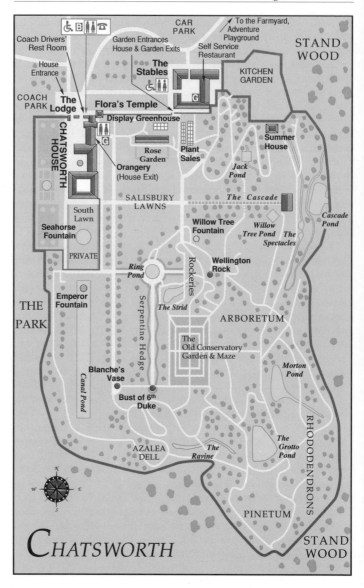

Coach Drivers'
Rest Room

CAR
PARK

To the Farmyard,
Adventure
Playground

STAND
WOOD

Garden Entrances
House & Garden Exits

Self Service
Restaurant

House
Entrance

**The
Stables**

KITCHEN
GARDEN

COACH
PARK

**The
Lodge**

Flora's Temple

Display Greenhouse

Summer
House

CHATSWORTH
HOUSE

**Rose
Garden**

**Plant
Sales**

*Jack
Pond*

Orangery
(House Exit)

SALISBURY
LAWNS

The Cascade

*Cascade
Pond*

South
Lawn

**Willow Tree
Fountain**

*Willow
Tree Pond*

*The
Spectacles*

**Seahorse
Fountain**

PRIVATE

*Ring
Pond*

**Wellington
Rock**

THE

**Emperor
Fountain**

Rockeries

THE
PARK

Serpentine Hedge

The Strid

ARBORETUM

*The
Old Conservatory
Garden & Maze*

*Morton
Pond*

**Blanche's
Vase**

Canal Pond

**Bust of 6ᵗʰ
Duke**

*The
Grotto
Pond*

AZALEA
DELL

*The
Ravine*

N

W   E

S

RHODODENDRONS

PINETUM

*C*HATSWORTH

STAND
WOOD

The highly decorative Painted Hall by Louis Laguerre

hang in the Victoria and Albert Museum in London. The carving over one of the doors has a military theme, consisting of swords, a drum, battle-axes, shield, helmet with a dragon crest etc. Over the other door is a similar theme and this is repeated on the mantel over the fireplace. Here there are cupids, trophies, masks, helmets, arms and two carved banners with the Cavendish arms, tied together with a snake (from the family crest). In the oval in the over mantel is a portrait of the first Duke. The ceiling called 'An Assembly of the Gods' is by Laguerre.

The next two rooms are somewhat similar. However, it is not the decoration for which the **State Music Room** is most remembered. In the same way that visitors to Plas Newydd on Anglesey remember the painting by Rex Whistler and its incredible footprints (they come towards you despite which end of the room you stand at), so visitors to Chatsworth always remember the violin. It hangs on the inner door to the gallery. Or does it? No, it is a painting by Jan Van der Vaart, but it has fooled countless visitors since it was placed here over 150 years ago. Again the carvings follow a theme — of foliage, flowers, fruit etc and the ceiling is again by Laguerre. Of the furniture in this room, the harpsichord dates from 1782 and the splendid malachite table, clock and urns were a gift from Czar Nicholas I, a friend of the Duke.

It is perhaps a little sad that the lovely old story about the violin is not true: it was held that the violin was painted by Verrio to deceive Grinling Gibbons, because the latter's carvings deceived people because of their delicate and lifelike image. However there is only one piece in the House by Gibbons; the rest are by the London carvers and Samuel Watson. What a shame!

Like the Music Room, the **State Bedroom** is lined with stamped and gilded leather. The ceiling is again by Laguerre. Now that it has been cleaned, it is clear to see how good he really was. The bed belonged to King George II. There are one or two items in the house which belonged to previous monarchs and became the perquisite of the fourth and sixth Dukes in their capacity of Lord Chamberlain.

The State Rooms are connected to the West Stairs by the **Sketch Gallery**. This gallery was built, like the south gallery, to enable access around the house without having to go through each room. It houses more tapestries woven at Mortlake together with portraits of all the Dukes and their Duchesses. The most stunning portrait is that of the present Duchess. It was painted by Pietro Annigoni in 1954. It draws one like a magnet. In a house full of portraits, it stands out like a beacon. Its strength is the almost photographic quality of Annigoni's work. It portrays in a unique way a most attractive woman.

The **West Stairs** house some recent sculptures in bronze by Angela Conner, including the current Duke. The ceiling, a little later than the work done by Laguerre in the State Rooms, is by Sir James Thornhill. The paintings, including one by Tintoretto and dating from the sixteenth century, distract the visitor before reaching the West Corridor and then the Chapel.

One can be forgiven for any desire to sit down in the **Chapel**. There is so much to absorb and unfortunately, the altar (unusually at the west end of the room) is at the end farthest away from the eye of discerning visitors. The room is virtually 48ft (15m) by 24ft (7m) and two stories in height. The room is most elegant and the marble carvings match the fine quality of the wood carvings on the walls. The four black marble pillars are in fact a form of limestone. It was quarried at Ashford near to Bakewell. The white stone is alabaster. Near to the black 'marble' deposits was found an unusual red limestone which became known as 'the Duke's red'. Examples of it may be seen from time to time. The whole deposit was worked out and stored in the cellars here at Chatsworth. The altar piece is incredibly fine craftsmanship. It was designed by Verrio, who painted the scene entitled 'Doubting Thomas'. The majority of the alabaster carving was left to Samuel Watson and the London carvers, although it had been designed by Caius Gabriel Cibber who carved the two flanking figures representing Faith and Justice. The cedar wainscotting gives the room its aroma. The wooden carvings were also done by Watson and his team. There are ten pendants flanking the cedar panels and two more either side of the altar. The work here was executed for the first Duke and remains largely unaltered. The upper walls were painted by Laguerre.

The contrast between the grandeur of the Chapel and the **Oak Room** could not be greater. The woodwork came from a German monastery and was purchased on a whim in a London auction! The remaining rooms to be seen are the Library and rooms in the west wing. They are approached through the Painted Hall and up the Oak Stairs. There are various paintings here, including one of the sixth Duke, who was responsible for the west wing. Here too is the only genuine example of work by Grinling Gibbons. It is in limewood and is of a lace cravat with a woodcock, leaves and Gibbon's trademark, a peapod. Traditionally, Gibbons carved the peapod open if he had received his commission in advance, otherwise it was carved closed. Here it is closed.

It reminds one of Lyme Hall, now a National Trust House at Disley, north-west of Buxton on the A6 trunk road. This was the home of the Legh family and several features at Chatsworth were

The State Music Room with the famous Trompe-l'oeil violin

The marble carvings and fine quality woodwork make the Chapel an irresistible attraction

Chatsworth House: the splendidly-carved Oak Room

repeated there. Lyme has its Gibbon's carving, including a peapod, which is open!

At the top of the stairs is the **Library**. Visitors only get a tantalising view into it. It is a little narrow being nearly 90ft (27m) long by 22ft (6m) wide, but has a most comfortable, interesting and relaxing appearance. What with the 14,000 volumes in this room, one could absorb time with ease here. The ceiling paintings are by Verrio. The Duchess in her book *The House* says 'It looks its best at night with the curtains drawn and the fire going, brass, mahogany, leather spines and gilt titles catching the light and making an atmosphere of comfort and calm'. What a splendid impression that leaves in one's mind as one approaches the Great Dining Room through the Ante Library and the Dome Room.

The **Great Dining Room** is an elegant room with a slight barrel-shaped ceiling, divided into hexagonal panels filled with roses and foliated flowers, richly covered with gold leaf. The room is hung with several Van Dyck portraits. The door surrounds are Ionic columns supporting alabaster entablatures. Of particular interest perhaps are the massive sidetables with their slab tops. The grey ones are Siberian Jasper and amongst the presents received from Tsar Nicholas I. The red ones are phophyritic sienite and the other two (there are six in all) are composite of hornblende and possibly calcite.

Upon leaving the room, there are a pair of vases made from Blue John stone. This is a coloured type of fluorspar mined near Castleton in the Peak District. The largest vase made out of a single piece of Blue John stone and nearly twenty inches in diameter is in the collection here. It was made by William Adam, a local geologist who also made ornaments from stone. He also wrote *Gem of the Peak* in the 1840s which includes a detailed description of Chatsworth House. The vase, known as the Chatsworth Tazza, may be seen on the table in the centre of the next large room, the **Sculpture Gallery**.

This is reached by passing from the Great Dining Room and then through the Vestibule with its gallery where the sixth Duke's private orchestra used to play. The Sculpture Gallery was built to house the sixth Duke's collection of sculptures. For years the room was a monument in itself to changes in taste and fashion. Now there is a revival of interest and the works of art housed here are becoming increasingly appreciated once more. A recent alteration, and a success, has been the hanging of red and green velvet on the walls. The room has a warmer feel to it than it had.

The final room in the tour of Chatsworth the **Orangery** which houses more carvings, the domestic State Coach and shop. The running costs of this huge house were once reported as being in the order of £1 million per annum: an immense sum to find. This has been addressed in various ways and the shop now sells various items manufactured under the Duchess of Devonshire's own brand label. Additionally, the Farm Shop at Pilsley sells meat and other produce (including venison) from the estate.

In order to protect the house and collection, attention was given to ensure its preservation. A charity was established which was the first in Britain to be granted a long lease of a country house and much of its collection. The object of the charity is the preservation of the house in perpetuity for the benefit of the public, thereby continuing the long tradition of opening the house to visitors.

Chatsworth Garden and Other Attractions

Very little of the Elizabethan house now survives and it is to the garden that one must turn for more tangible remains. The **Hunting Tower**, recently refurbished, continues to look over the park and has an upper floor moulded-plaster ceiling by Abraham Smith. The Sea Horse Fountain between the south front and the canal pond is of this early period but the formal gardens were removed to create the natural parkland of Capability Brown. By the bridge is Queen Mary's Bower, where the ill-fated Scottish Queen was allowed to take fresh air and perhaps contemplate her ultimate fate.

The first Duke's Greenhouse is now a camellia house with rose beds laid out in front of it. Between here and the cascades are the large Salisbury Lawns now over 250 years old. They have never been treated with chemicals and exhibit a richness and variety of herbs that is missed by the casual visitor. The **Cascades** and **Cascade House** at the top were also left by Brown. Today they are a favourite attraction of many young visitors who paddle and play here on the balmy days of summer. The water comes from the system of lakes on the moors above. The **Emperor Lake** also feeds water through cast iron pipes to the **Emperor Fountain** in the **Canal Pond**. This was built for Emperor Tsar Nicholas I who was expected here in 1844 while on a state visit. It rose to a height of 267ft (81m). It is not played to its full capacity these days because of erosion to the banks of the pond. The highest jet the fountain is recorded as reaching is 296ft (90m), a record for a gravity-fed system. Incidentally the Tsar was also expected at Harewood where improvements had equally been effected ahead of the visit.

Adjacent to the first Duke's greenhouse is the modern **greenhouse**. It is a worthy successor the Paxton's massive greenhouse which was blown up between the wars. It had housed palms and other hot-house plants which had died through lack of attention

The magnificent Emperor Fountain

The Hunting Tower is four storeys high and commands a marvellous view across the Derwent Valley

This fountain can be seen at the top of the cascade in Chatsworth Garden

during the Great War, when the gardeners answered the call to arms. The *Victoria regia* lily (Amazon Lily) had first flowered in cultivated form at Chatsworth in 1849. Today it grows again in the split-level hot house along with mangos, bread fruit and other tropical plants. Unfortunately it is not possible to open this feature to the public, but it is nice to think that the botanical sensation of nearly a century and a half ago has a contemporary connection.

The gardens are enormous (they extend to 105 acres) and plenty of time should be allowed to explore them. Try and pick up the leaflet on the Stand Wood walks and buy the guidebook to the garden. Worth looking out for is the site of Paxton's **greenhouse**. It contains a yew tree maze which is open to the public in the summer and a large bed of lupins, resplendent in many colours in June and July. The structure of the greenhouse has gone but the side walls remain. So does, incidentally, the large underground boiler house, chimney flues and the line of a short underground railway which brought coal to the boilers.

Higher up the garden is the willow tree fountain. Look out for the enormous fish nearby and a massive pivoted stone, now locked in the open position.

With its carefully tended lawns and borders, clipped yews and statuary, this is a garden for all seasons. Early in the year, the walks to the ponds from the Hunting Tower are a mass of bluebells. Rhododendrons and azaleas add colour to both the garden and woodlands too. The laburnum tunnel brings a riot of yellow to the garden as the herbaceous borders also come into bloom.

North of the garden are three of the various other attractions at Chatsworth. Paine's enormous stable block now houses the café and restaurant facilities plus a number of shops set around the courtyard.

✳ Behind the Stables is the **Farmyard** and **Adventure Playground**. The former has a collection of various farm animals, bygone farm-yard implements, a woodlands feature and large fish-breeding tanks. It is a popular feature with children. Older children may find more of interest in the large Adventure Playground in its woodland setting. Just before the entrance to the Farmyard is a dog pound in case you prefer not to leave your dog in the car. It is also where the Stand Wood walks begin.

✳ At the southern end of the park is the Calton Lees car park. Many visitors like to park here and walk upriver to Chatsworth. Just beyond the car park is the **Chatsworth Garden Centre**. It sells everything from plants to pictures, fencing to food. Opened only a few years ago it has already developed into a popular venue. The road from here to Chatsworth continues northwards through

Edensor to Baslow with a turning off to the left to **Pilsley**. This village was built to house the first wave of relocated Edensor residents, moved so that the rural tranquillity of Chatsworth could be improved. Here is the estate Farm Shop. It sells produce from the estate and there are several other craft workshops located here.

In **Baslow**, The Cavendish Hotel, run by the estate, contains many furnishings from the house. This is definitely an upmarket hotel offering high standard accommodation, food and service. It is the successor to a number of hotels built by previous Dukes around the Peak District such as The Crescent in Buxton.

Beyond Chatsworth House and its garden, the nearby village of **Edensor** is a justifiably popular venue. It houses the rest of the residents of Edensor's old village who did not move to Pilsley. The old village site can be clearly seen for one solitary house remained, surrounded by its high stone wall, just to the north of the entrance to the Chatsworth drive at Edensor. In front of it, the location of the former village street can be discerned. It appears that the occupant owned his freehold and refused to sell to the Duke who had no option but to accept the situation!

Various designs were drawn up for the new village. They varied from Italianate to more traditional architecture. Whether the Duke intended to have one of each is not known, but that is what was finally decided. All the properties are different and how pleasing the result. Edensor is dominated by its nineteenth-century church, standing above the village, its tall spire emphasising the dominance.

An early victim of Irish troubles was Lord Frederick Cavendish who was assasinated in Phoenix Park, Dublin. He is buried in Edensor churchyard and the everlasting flowers sent by Queen Victoria to the funeral may still be seen. Also buried here is Kathleen Kennedy, who died in an aircrash in 1948. She would have been the Duchess had both she and her husband lived. He died in action in France during the war. She was the sister of President John F. Kennedy and he visited Chatsworth to see his sister's grave when he was President. He was in Britain as the guest of Prime Minister Macmillan who was the current Duke's uncle. The Cavendish family had represented West Derbyshire in Parliament for generations. As Marquis of Hartington, Kathleen's husband had contested the election during World War II. He was defeated, an early indicator of the shock which awaited Winston Churchill in 1946. Lord Hartington returned to the war and was killed shortly afterwards. One suspects that these reminders of such sad events in the Cavendish family are far from the minds of the throngs of visitors who stroll around this attractive little village today.

The decorative façade of the Stables

*Bakewell Church
includes the largest
and most varied
group of medieval
monuments in the
United Kingdom*

Edensor

Across the main road at Edensor is the former Chatsworth Inn. This handsome Georgian property is now the Estate Office. Close to the cattle grid across the road near to this building is a clearly seen footpath which connects Edensor with Chatsworth itself only a few minutes away, but completely hidden from view at this point.

Additional Information

Places to Visit at Chatsworth

Chatsworth

Open: the fields on the west side of the River Derwent are available for you to wander at will, but please respect the livestock and keep dogs on a lead. The house is open daily from April to the end of October, 11am-4.30pm. The garden is open for an extra half hour, until 5pm. Directions: Chatsworth is signposted from junction 29 of the M1. Use the A619 and just follow the white on brown signs all the way to the house. It is 16 miles (26km). From the M6, it is 36 miles (58km) and from junction 29. The nearest railway station is Chesterfield which is twenty minutes away.

Farmyard and Adventure Playground

Live animals; milking demonstration daily at 3.30pm. Exciting Adventure Playground. Shop and Tea Room. The Farmyard and Adventure Playground are open from April to end of September, 10.30am-4.30pm. The Adventure Playground only is open in October, and then on Saturdays and Sundays only. ☎ 0246 583139 or ☎ 0246 582204, Ext 365.

The Carriage House Restaurant

In the east range of James Paine's stable block built in 1764, is a self-service and fully licensed restaurant, serving home-made food. Seating for 250. Open 10.15am-5.30pm. Party bookings accepted. ☎ 0246 582204, ext 364

Chatsworth Shops: The Orangery and The Carriage House Shop

Gifts, many selected by the Duchess of Devonshire and based on designs from the House and Garden; produce, stationery, books and much more. ☎ 0246 582204

Potting Shed

In the Garden
Home grown plants, fruit and vegetables as available.

Chatsworth Estate Farm Shop

Stud Farm, Pilsley (1½ miles/2km from House)
Meat, game, dairy produce, cheese, home-made sausages, bread, cakes, ice cream and fudge. English wines and beers and other specialities. ☎ 0246 583392. Coffee Shop.

Stud Farm Craft Workshops

Pilsley
Next to the Farm Shop. Open to visitors. Broome's Barns Workshops, Pilsley Penrose and Rietberg, upholsterers. ☎ 0246 583444

Chatsworth Garden Centre

Calton Lees (1¼ miles from house)
Large selection of house plants, hardy

nursery stock and garden sundries.
☎ 0629 734004

Chatsworth Forestry
Calton Lees, next to Garden Centre.
Manufacturers of tanalised fencing
stakes, gates, post and rail fencing,
and horse jumps. Delivery and
erection service available.
☎ 0629 732316

Useful Information: Chatsworth

Services and Information
For information on the house and
special events write to Chatsworth,
Bakewell, Derbyshire, DE45 1PP, or
☎ 0246 582204. There is a 24-hour
service on the telephone. Fax: 0246
583536. A 'Friends of Chatsworth'
scheme exists for regular visitors,
with a money-saving season ticket
for regular visitors.
Catering: is available on the estate
at the Stable Block and the Garden
Centre (at Calton Lees).

Chatsworth Park Caravan Club Site
118 touring caravan pitches in an old
walled garden. April to October.
To book ☎ 0246 582226

Special Events
Chatsworth hosts an Angling Fair
in May and caters for game, coarse
and sea fishing enthusiasts, with
added family attractions. For
Trout fishing on the River Wye.
☎ 0629 640484

Country Fair
This two day spectacular is held in
September. In addition to 150 trade
stands there are massed pipe and
military bands, hot air balloons,
and free fall parachuting. This
weekend the house and garden are
open to Country Fair visitors only.

Disabled Visitors
Wheelchairs are welcome in the
garden, restaurant and shops, but
not the house because the tour
involves various staircases. Two
wheelchairs are available at the
Garden entrance. Dogs are
welcome in the garden and there is
a dog pound near to the Farmyard.

Other Places to Visit

Bakewell
Old House Museum
Cunningham Place
Off Church Lane, Bakewell
☎ 0629 813647
Open: Good Friday to end of October
daily 2-5pm. Folk museum in early
sixteenth-century house.

Bakewell Church
Dates from Norman, possibly
Saxon period. Largest collection of
medieval monuments in the United
Kingdom, found during nine-
teenth-century restoration work.

Buxton
*The Crescent/Opera House and
    Pavilion Gardens Complex*
Town centre group of buildings
worthy of a visit. ☎ 0298 78662

Crich
National Tramway Museum
Follow signs from A6 to Cromford.
The national collection of over forty
fully restored old trams. ☎ 0773 852565
Open: April to end September daily
(except some out of season Fridays).

Cromford Village
Local history trail around early
industrial community. Arkwright's
mill and Cromford Canal Wharf.

Arkwright's Mill
Mill Lane, Cromford
The world's earliest water-powered
cotton-spinning mill. Displays and

refreshments, car parking at Cromford Wharf, opposite. ☎ 0629 824297
Open: daily 9.30am-5pm except 25 December.

Disley
Lyme Hall & Park
Stockport SK12 2NX
☎ 0663 762023
Open: Good Friday, April to October. Closed Monday and Friday except Bank Holiday Monday. Guided tours weekdays and Saturdays. Last admissions 4pm (tours), 4.15pm. Special Christmas openings, please telephone for details.
Garden: Open all year daily except 25 &26 December. Summer April to October 11am-5pm; Winter 4 October to Good Friday 1994, 11am-4pm. Shop in hall open same time as Hall.

Haddon Hall
Situated on the A6, 2 miles (3km) south of Bakewell
☎ 0629 812855
Open: late March to beginning of October, daily except Mondays (and Sundays in July and August 11am-6pm).
Totally unspoilt medieval and Tudor manor house with beautiful rose garden on terraces above the River Wye.

Lea
Lea Gardens
In Lea village, near Cromford, proceed uphill under Smedley's Mill overhead footway or 'bridge' for 1½ miles (2km), turn right on sharp bend. Over 500 varieties of rhododendrons in woodland setting. Well worth visiting in May to July.

Matlock Bath
Peak District Lead Mining Museum
The Pavilion
Displays on the ancient lead

mining industry of the Peak District. Includes a rare and very large hydraulic pumping engine dating from 1819.
Open: daily except Christmas Day 11am-4pm (later closing in summer).
☎ 0629 583834

Rowsley
Cauldwell's Mill
Situated just off the A6 in centre of village.
Nineteenth-century water turbine driven corn rolling mill. Craft Centre.
Open: March to October daily 10am-6pm. Winter weekends 10am-4.30pm.

Tourist Information Centres

Ashbourne
13 Market Place
☎ 0335 343666
Open: March to October daily 9.30am-5.30pm, Sundays July and August only. November to February Monday to Saturday 10am-4pm.

Bakewell
Old Market Hall
Bridge Street
Bakewell ☎ 0629 813227
Open: March to October Monday to Friday 9.30am-5.30pm, Saturday and Sunday 9.30am-6pm. November to February Friday to Wednesdays 9.30am-5pm, Thursdays 9.30am-1pm.

Matlock Bath
The Pavilion
Matlock Bath
☎ 0629 55082
Open: March to October daily 9.30am-5.30pm. November to February Wednesdays to Mondays 10am-4pm (Saturdays 9.30am-4.30pm). Closed Tuesdays.

Accommodation and Eating Out

A full list of accommodation in the area is available from Bakewell Tourist Information Centre. A 48-hour booking service operates from the three tourist information centres run by Derbyshire Dales District Council. The addresses are given under the Tourist Information Centres section.

In addition to the hotels many local pubs offer food. The Devonshire Arms in Beely, just south of Chatsworth enjoys a good reputation. Do not overlook the facilities at Chatsworth refered to above. Ther are numerous cafés and restaurants in Bakewell, to suit most tastes.

HOTELS

Baslow
Cavendish Hotel
Derbyshire DE4 1SP
☎ 0246 582311. Fax: 0246 582312
Expensive.

Devonshire Arms
Derbyshire DE4 1SR
☎ 0246 582551. Fax: 0246 582116
Medium range.

Bakewell
Rutland Arms Hotel
Rutland Square, Bakewell
Derbyshire DE4 1BT
☎ 0629 812812. Fax: 0629 812309
Medium range.

Over Haddon
The Lathkill Hotel
Nr Bakewell, Derbyshire
☎ 0629 812501
Small cosy pub with dramatic views into Lathkill Dale. Restaurant available for non residents.

Rowsley
Peacock Hotel
Nr Matlock, Derbyshire DE4 2EB
☎ 0629 733518. Fax: 0629 732671
Expensive.

BED & BREAKFAST

Alport
Rock House
Nr Bakewell, Derbyshire
☎ 0629 636736
Situated off the road to Youlgreave off the A6 south of Bakewell.

Ashbourne
Overdale
Lode Lane, Alstonfield
Ashbourne, Derbyshire
☎ 0335 27206 or 275
A friendly welcome in a pretty, very popular limestone village. The nearby George Inn is the archetypal rural English Inn, very welcoming and popular with walkers.

The Old House
Church Street, Ashbourne
Derbyshire
☎ 0335 343240
A Georgian house between the thirteenth-century church and the Mansion House. Recent second floor adaptation to a high standard.

Belper
The Hollins
45 Belper Lane
Belper, Derbyshire
☎ 0773 823955
A warm, friendly house pleasantly situated off the A6 between Derby and Matlock Bath. Convenient for people travelling from the south off junction 29 of the M1. 16 miles (26 km) from Chatsworth.

7

HAREWOOD HOUSE

Situated off the busy A61 between Harrogate and Leeds is Harewood House. One suspects that few people glance into the estate village as they rush past. On the opposite side of the road, hidden from view lies Harewood House. Its presence is well marked; the large and imposing entrance arch and stone boundary wall, 9 miles (14km), in length herald the house beyond.

Looking at the north front as one approaches the house its importance and history including that of its post-war years, is not that apparent. Yet the excellent state of repair gives a clue. Despite crippling post-war death duties and the sale of a few of the treasures, prudent management, foresight and perhaps some good luck have been its saviour. Had these qualities not attended the work of the current seventh Earl of Harewood, the house may well have been an antiseptic place, devoid of its family and its priceless collection.

It is the collection and the work of Robert Adam that is the main attraction here. The house has the largest private picture gallery in this country, if not Europe, the best collection of Chippendale furniture anywhere and some of the best work of Adam. Victorian alterations by Sir Charles Barry destroyed some of Adam's work and left other rooms in an altered condition. However by good fortune, the carvings and filigree work of Chippendale and Adam which Barry removed had survived 150 years of storage.

The current Earl knew that the removed items had been put into store. A search at his instigation uncovered a priceless treasure, not only of the filigree removed from the huge Chippendale mirrors hanging in the house, but of additional matching mirrors! The decision to restore these to the house impacted on other rooms in addition to the Gallery and a major restoration work was the result. Today, after a long and careful period of work, the principal State

Rooms have been returned to something like their Adam style. They are resplendent in their fresh colours, Chippendale furniture and mirrors and the works of art from the family collection.

The story of Harewood however begins in the eighteenth century. Henry Lascelles purchased the Gawthorpe Estate in 1738. The manor house stood between the current house and the lake, but no visible traces remain above ground level. Henry's son Edwin, on his father's death, decided to rebuild his house on higher ground. He employed John Carr of York as his architect. Work started first on the stables in 1755, and the foundations of the house were laid in 1759. It was 1771 before it was occupied although work continued, especially on the Gallery.

Adam was invited in 1759 to look at Carr's plans and he made certain amendments to the structure, not all of which were in the end carried out. Internally, however, Adam had a free hand. What is remarkable about Harewood is that much of his work and influence remains, despite the Victorian alterations. His designs for ceilings, walls, friezes and carpets are unmistakeable. The work of many of his collaborative craftsmen and decorative painters remains in abundance. Additional to the majestic form of the ceiling decorations, one of the beauties of Harewood House are the painted panels by Antonio Zucchi, Biagio Rebecca and Angelica Kaufmann. However some may not be Kaufmann's; much is in her style but after recent research, only a couple of panels are definitely attributed to her — there is no documentary proof that she was ever here. Lord Harewood is sanguine about his Kaufmanns, or the sudden lack of them. In a few years maybe someone will reappraise the artist and announce that he has a lot more again!

What is not in dispute is the work of Thomas Chippendale. He was brought in to give life to the rooms. Like Adam, his ideas were at the forefront of interior design. His furniture here is exquisite. In fact the Dining Room sideboards and the pedestals with urns which flank one of them are now considered to be amongst the finest furniture ever made. Perhaps his finest piece however is the commode in Princess Mary's Sitting Room. It cost Edwin Lascelles £86 and is certainly Chippendale's most famous work. Chippendale's work at Harewood cost over £6,500. Coincidentally, it was matched by the cost of work of Capability Brown outside the house.

As the house was completed, Edwin Lascelles could turn his attention to his grounds. Gawthorpe was pulled down and Capability Brown was brought in to provide the setting seen today. Despite the loss of 10,000 mature trees in the 1962 gales much of what is here is attributable to him. An essential difference is that the grass went

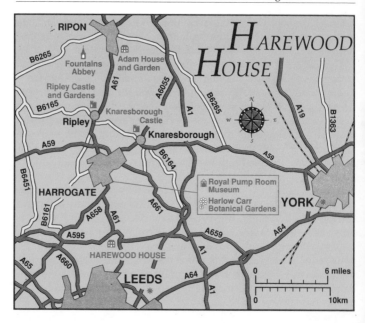

The north façade which was redesigned by Sir Charles Barry

The south front was transformed with the addition of Sir Charles Barry's Victorian Terrace

up to the house on the south front, as it still does on the north side. The terrace was one of Barry's additions. It is difficult these days to visualise that the apparently natural features we see today are artificial. The vistas Brown created were of course, all in his mind. He had passed away long before his trees reached maturity.

Much of the building today reflects the house altered by Sir Charles Barry in the 1840s. Barry was brought to Harewood by Louisa, Lady Harewood who was married to the third Earl. He is perhaps best known as the architect of the Houses of Parliament and of the Reform Club in London. His work at Harewood was to be significant. The house lost its classical columns and pediment on the south front, and the huge terrace was added. The terrace is a very strong feature of that side of the house and the effect is pleasing. With the flight of steps up to the State Rooms, it seems to link the house with the grounds most successfully. Barry added an extra floor to the central block and to the two wings.

Barry also altered the interior and removed some of Adam's fixtures. Fortunately, they were kept in packing cases, lying half forgotten for 150 years. Restoration of these features has given an opportunity to restore some of the rooms to their previous Adam appearance. Great pains were taken to be as authentic as possible. One room which remains largely as Barry had altered it (except for its fireplace, now restored to its pre-Barry position in the Gallery) is the Dining Room. It is the room adjacent to the Gallery on the north front. It makes for an interesting comparison between the changing tastes of the Georgian and early Victorian eras.

The **Dining Room** is situated near the north entrance where a visit to the house begins. Here you can buy a guide book recommended and the cassette tape and head phones are a must. The voice is that of the Earl himself and the dialogue is terrific. Appreciating that we like to see a family in our stately homes, Lord Harewood guides you around his home, pointing out family detail, the things he most likes and remembers. The **Entrance Hall** is large and the guide book says that Adam conceived it as an ante-chamber rather than a place to linger. The intricate detail of the bas relief work by William Collins and the friezes are a good indication of the splendours elsewhere in the house.

In the centre of the room is a huge alabaster carving of *Adam* (not the architect!) by Jacob Epstein. One suspects that most visitors will either love it or hate it. As the guide book succinctly puts it 'the degree to which Epstein's Adam fits into Robert Adam's overall decorative scheme may intrigue the visitor'.

The tour starts in the **Old Library**. However it is not the books which make this room so pleasing; it is the wall paintings by Biagio Rebecca, the bas relief work and of course the ceiling and frieze united with the room as a whole by the Corinthian pilasters. The whole creates a wonderful start to the tour.

The next room is the **China Room**. Part of the house collection of Sèvres is housed here. Take a close look at some of the finest china ever manufactured. There is also a cabinet containing the Stone Coquerel et le Gros service which was a gift from Queen Mary to her daughter Princess Mary. The plates have interesting views of British churches and country houses, some now demolished such as Clumber. However it is the Sèvres which perhaps lingers longest in one's memory.

Proceeding through Princess Mary's Dressing Room one enters the **East Bedroom** which was where Edwin Lascelles slept. There is a nice touch here on the tape where the Earl describes a moment when Princess Mary was also using this room and the four poster bed. From here, the tour proceeds down the east front of the house through various minor rooms and the East Dressing Room which has some interesting paintings of Italian views by Cromek who lived in Leeds.

On the south-east corner of the house is Lord Harewood's **Sitting Room**. The Earl describes this as 'a cheerful, unpretentious room'. It is indeed that, but most pleasing to eye nonetheless. It is hung with various family portraits including a charcoal drawing of Princess Mary by John Sargent, drawn in 1925. Apparently Princess Mary did not like it.

On through an ante room one reaches **Princess Mary's Sitting Room**. The room is superb in itself, highlighted with Ionian columns either side of a recess. The delicacy of Adam's plasterwork should not be overlooked. However it is the furniture here which is of particular interest. The two commodes and secretaire are perhaps Thomas Chippendale's finest pieces of furniture and rank as some of the finest pieces of furniture anywhere. It is perhaps not too wild a claim that together with the Dining Room sideboards and pedestals, the house has the finest English furniture ever made, probably one of the best collections in the world.

The room houses an impressive collection of watercolours of the house, by some of the finest landscape artists. Here hang works by Girtin, Malton, Turner and Varley. This breathtaking room is followed by the **Spanish Library**. The title of 'Spanish Library' comes from the leather covering on the walls above the book cases. The room was the State Dressing Room and Queen Victoria stayed in this room when she visited Harewood at the age of 15 in 1834.

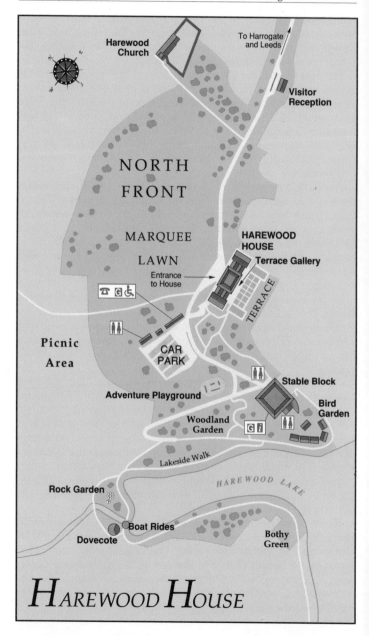

Harewood
Church

To Harrogate
and Leeds

Visitor
Reception

NORTH
FRONT

MARQUEE

LAWN

HAREWOOD
HOUSE

Terrace Gallery

Entrance
to House

TERRACE

Picnic
Area

CAR
PARK

Stable Block

Adventure Playground

Bird
Garden

Woodland
Garden

Lakeside Walk

HAREWOOD LAKE

Rock Garden

Boat Rides

Dovecote

Bothy
Green

Harewood House

The colourful Chinese 'famille verté' vases in the Entrance Hall

The Entrance Hall with Jacob Epstein's alabaster carving of Adam

The next room is the **Library**, a large room with ceiling decoration by Adam. It is spectacular, complementing his overmantels above the fireplaces. They have delicately carved roundels reflecting superb craftsmanship. The heavy book-cases are Barry's. The room in a way prepares you for the breathtaking Yellow Drawing Room and the Cinnamon Drawing Room which follow it. The restoration of these two rooms has been particularly successful and one needs time to absorb the intricate original craftsmanship let alone the recent redecoration.

Great pains have been expended to try and recreate Adam's original colour scheme in the **Yellow Drawing Room**. Investigation of original design documents and paint scrapes were made before the final decorative scheme was decided. Note that the carpet follows the general design of the ceiling. The Chippendale mirror reflects the various Meissen animals on the mantelpiece. The remaining china is Sèvres and includes a magnificent vase on the left side of the room. The paintings include some of the family ancestors, including one of Lawrence's of the Prime Minister, George Canning. Some of the works here were left to the current Earl's father by his uncle, the Marquess of Clanricarde. The bequest included a number of paintings together with a considerable fortune which was used to finance the acquisition of many of the Italian paintings in the collection.

The **Cinnamon Drawing Room** follows, in which hang family portraits including seven by Sir Joshua Reynolds. There are others by some of the best eighteenth- and nineteenth-century portrait painters, including Sir Thomas Lawrence and Thomas Gainsborough. The Victorians removed a lot of the filigree work around the Chippendale pier glasses (the large mirrors) and indeed even put some of the mirrors into store. Recent restoration work included a painstaking refurbishment of the two mirrors in this room, bringing back the filigree which had been carefully stored for 150 years. The mirrors were then united with the Chippendale pier tables, just as they had originally been. As you walk through this room, look carefully at the recent paintwork around the windows. The intricate pattern of different paints shows very clearly what a complicated process the restoration work has involved.

The **Gallery** runs the full width of the house, from the north front to the south. It has recently been restored very much as it was in Adam's day, and most of the alterations made by Barry have been removed. The original fireplace which Barry moved to the Dining Room, has been restored. He had also removed the columns in the Venetian windows and reduced the effect of the wooden pelmets, made by Chippendale and intended originally to be the only 'curtains' in the room. The wallpaper was specially made recently for the room and is based upon a design used at Nostell Priory. Despite floods from rooms above and a fire, the ceiling is original and probably cleaned but never re-painted. The walls are hung with the Italian collection made by the present Earl's father. The two statues are nineteenth century and not only finish off the view but catch the eye when viewed down the enfilade of the rooms leading to the Gallery. The furniture is by Chippendale. Today the room is used regularly for musical performances, a role for which it is now particularly well suited.

The tour leaves the Gallery for the **Dining Room**, a creation of Barry's. Here hangs portraits of all the owners of Harewood with the exception of the current Earl, and three of their wives, including the portrait of Princess Mary over the fireplace — a gift from the Harewood tenants to her husband upon the occasion of their marriage in 1922. Although Adam's structural design has been lost his impact on the room's furniture remains. The chairs are by Chippendale, as are the sideboard, wine coolers and pedestals (which house plate warmers and silver chests). Here is some of the finest of English furniture.

The final room on the tour, prior to returning to the Entrance Hall once more, is the **Music Room**. This room is one of the least changed from Adam's concept. The wall paintings and ceiling roundels are by Antonio Zucchi, the chairs, sofas and frame to the painting by Sir Joshua Reynolds over the fireplace are all by Chippendale. The china is from the Sèvres collection, which was created by Edward Lascelles in 1802. Notice too how once again the carpet mirrors the ceiling design.

Despite the ravages of time and Victorian alteration, the current Earl and Countess, along with their immediate predecessors, successfully restored their home to reflect the original work of Robert Adam. Together with its collection of Chippendale furniture, its large picture and china collection, it has survived the ravages of Death Duties remarkably well. It is truly one of the finest Treasure Houses in England.

Attractions at Harewood

A gateway on the way from the car park to the Stables gives access to the Terrace, the Italianate garden and to the Terrace Gallery. If you are visiting in the spring, look out for the huge peonies which grow below the terrace wall. A path runs down towards the Stables inside

Chippendale's famous 'Diana and Minerva' commode in the Princess Mary's Sitting Room

The Old Library

the railings so that you may avoid the roadway. It wends its way down through specimen trees and shrub beds. The house comes back into view at the bottom, close to the Stables.

Beyond the latter, a path gives access to the woodland walk which leads you down to the lake. You will notice a considerable number of rhododendrons. The storm of 1962, which destroyed so many trees here created gaps in the canopy which allowed the planting of rhododendrons. Many species and hybrids had been planted earlier reflecting the interest of the sixth Earl and the Princess Royal. Today there are some 150 or so different varieties, catalogued and given a number by which to identify them. A useful guide may be obtained from the Estate Office, complete with a location plan. Mid-May is

The Music Room is a splendid example of Robert Adams 'decorative scheme' at which he consistently aimed

perhaps the best time to see them, some varieties flower later (or earlier) which spreads the Harewood flowering season.

The woodland path follows the lake round the dam and waterfall and then to the Bothy, where the path ends and where there is a garden of old-fashioned roses. Close to the dovecote waterfall are the rock garden and azalea beds. There are daily half-hour boat rides on the lake adjacent to the dovecote waterfall.

The **Terrace Gallery** is reached only from the terrace. It is beneath the State Rooms and is used for exhibitions of contemporary art and furniture which are changed regularly. Look out for details of the current exhibition or ask at the reception desk when you enter the house.

The **Stables** now houses an excellent cafeteria. There are tables so that you may sit in the colonnaded courtyard on a sunny day. A functions suite is available for seminars and weddings.

Access to the **Bird Garden** is from the Stable Courtyard. It occupies the ground between the Stables and the lake and is well worth a visit. A lot of effort has been put into the displays and the garden in which it is situated. The variety of birds is unexpected, as is the tropical house. There are some 600 birds ranging from the popular Humbolt Penguins and Chilean Flamingoes (which breed here) to the exceedingly rare Waldrapp Ibis. Harewood is the home of the Northern Collection of the World Pheasant Association. However, it is not only pheasants which are the focus of conservation attention here. There is a strong educational interest to any visit and Harewood's conservation work comes across clearly.

A feature is the **Tropical House** containing tropical plants and birds kept at a minimum temperature of 75°F (24°C). A sprinkler system keeps the atmosphere humid. Some of the birds in here are tiny, especially the delightful humming birds. Palm trees, bamboo and other plants create an authentic atmosphere of threatened landscape. On leaving the Tropical House you may see the food preparation display, featuring different diets, from fruit, seed and pellets to Grimsby fish for the penguins.

There are two other buildings at Harewood worthy of note — the church and the castle. The **castle** is medieval and was already a ruin when the building work on the new house was undertaken. A painting of it by J. M. W. Turner in 1798 gives a good idea of what it looked like at that time. Two large towers had gone and in fact, the building was described as being 'much decayed' when the estate was sold in 1656, 140 years prior to Turner's painting. In fact it was described as being a useful source of building material (dressed stone and timber) for the adjacent village of Harewood. The ruins are situated close to the main road, to the north of Harewood village.

The fifteenth-century **All Saints Church** is in the Park. It was, prior to the Reformation, owned by the Augustinian priory at Bolton Abbey near Ilkley. Subsequent alterations resulted in the loss of much of the medieval stained glass and the wooden furnishings of the period such as seats, stalls and screen. However, luckily for us, beneath the perpendicular architecture associated with the late medieval period are a remarkable collection of alabaster carved tombs of the fifteenth century. They are associated with previous Lords of the Manor and escaped the vagaries of time and alternative religious zest. The tomb chests are highly carved and portray the costumes of the time, the oldest one dating from 1429. Look carefully for traces of the original paint, red on the robe and green on the underlining of this oldest monument. The effigy is of Sir William Gascoigne, Lord Chief Justice of England. Shakespeare refers to him in *Henry VI* as the judge who imprisoned the future King Henry V.

The current furnishings of the church, together with the stained glass (except for a few medieval fragments) date from the restoration undertaken by Sir Giles Gilbert Scott in 1862-63. In 1978, the church was declared redundant and taken into the care of the Redundant Churches Fund. The fabric is conserved, along with the monuments, which, insofar as was possible, were returned to their original locations. The church is open to visitors and a visit is recommended.

Harewood has a full annual programme of special events which cover the spring season. It includes several musical features, especially open-air classical concerts, catering for the whole family; simply come with warm clothes and a car blanket, sit in the park and enjoy the music — and sometimes a closing firework display. Other special events include car rallies and a traction engine rally, the Harewood Show, Game and Craft Fairs. Full details are available from the Estate Office.

Harrogate

Six miles (10km) to the north of Harewood is Harrogate. It became popular in Victorian times as a fashionable spa town. Agatha Christie's famous 10 day 'dissapearance' in 1926 was made into a book and film entitled *Agatha*, and was filmed in Harrogate (1978). Today, the Royal Pump Room Museum and the Royal Baths Assembly Rooms remind one of the days when people came to 'take the waters'. A further reminder, and an important aspect of the town's continuing popularity are the many Victorian shops and hotels. The Majestic Hotel looking down onto the centre and the Conference

Centre. It retains sufficient of its Victorian past to be interesting, even quaint in some respects, but modernised and comfortable where it matters. The Old Swan and The Crown are similar except the latter lacks a decent sized car park in this motorised age.

Harrogate is today an important conference centre, which means it is advantageous to book accommodation early. It has an advantage for tourists however. The Tourist Board Accommodation List gives over two hundred places to stay in the town, plus dozens more nearby! It is described as one of the most attractive towns in Britain. It is reminiscent of the smaller town of Buxton in Derbyshire, north-west of Chatsworth and built also as a spa by an early Duke of Devonshire. Harrogate is described as England's Floral Town. The area of Prospect and Crescent Gardens and Montpellier Crescent are

The Gallery

The lake and bridge above the waterfall are among the features seen on the lakeside walk

A sphinx on the south front Terrace

lovely places to stroll around in summer when they are bedecked with flowers. The Tourist Board is located in the Royal Baths Assembly Rooms. Here a variety of different cures could be obtained and the Turkish Baths are open seven days a week.

Nearby is the Royal Pump Room Museum. It was built in 1842 and here the Victorians congregated to drink the mineral water from the old sulphur well. The building had been restored and is conspicuous with its copper dome. It is now a museum charting the history of the town and also records the history of Harrogare as a spa town. The mineral water whose healing qualities made the town famous still bubble up to the surface and may be sampled as in former times.

Encircling the town centre is the Stray, a huge open area where one may relax and watch the world go by. The beautiful Valley Gardens has thirty-six different mineral wells and hosts the Spring Flower Show each April. There are amenities here for children and tennis courts. Garden lovers will be particularly interested in the Harlow Carr Botanical Gardens, which cover 68 acres. This is the home of the Northern Horticultural Society and specialises in growing plants which are suited to a northern climate. It is open all the year around and has a restaurant, gift shop and plant sales department.

North of Harrogate are the limestone dales (or valleys) of the **Yorkshire Dales National Park**. This is justifiably a popular area — a beautiful region, not only in its dales, but with its compact ancient villages and solemn grandeur of its ruined monasteries. It was popular long before a local vet put his pen to paper and introduced the world to the life of James Herriot. It is worthy of at least several days exploration. Indeed, a visit to Yorkshire should encompass a visit to York and Castle Howard (see chapter 8).

A visit to the Yorkshire Dales should include a trip to **Fountains Abbey** and **Studley Royal** near Ripon. Now owned by the National Trust, the abbey remains are the most complete in England and are incorporated in the park of Studley Royal. The abbey dates from 1132, but the park is a large eighteenth-century landscaped garden, centred on a lake. Together they combine to make a marvellous excursion.

Additional Information

Places to Visit

Harewood House
Open: gates open daily 10am.
House opens at 11am. Last
admission 4.30pm. Open approximately April to the end of October,
specific opening and closing days
may vary.
Directions: Harewood is situated 7
miles (11km) north of Leeds on the
A61 to Harrogate. It is 22 miles
(35km) from York and 5 miles
(8km) from Wetherby. If you are
approaching from the M1, upon
reaching the end of the motorway
at Leeds, simply follow all signs for
Harrogate, A61. They lead you
straight through the centre of town
but usually clear of delays. Leeds is
served by train and there is a bus
service to Harewood every
30 minutes from central Leeds and
Harrogate.

Services and Information
The address is Harewood House,
Harewood, Leeds, LS17 9LQ
☎ (0532) 886331. Correspondence
should be addressed to the Estate
Office, which has a 24-hour
answering service giving details of
opening times and latest information on special exhibitions and
forthcoming events.

Education Services
Study visits by groups of all ages
are encouraged. A teacher's
planning pack, resource materials
and a fully equipped classroom are
available. Guided tours of the
house are available to groups on
special request. The use of the
walkman tape, with a commentary
by the Earl, is particularly recommended.

*Corporate Entertainment and Special
Occasions*
Harewood provides a unique
setting for very special occasions,
product launches and quality
corporate entertaining such as State
Dining Room dinners and Gallery
banqueting. Requirements may be
discussed with the Marketing
Manager ☎ (0532) 886331. For
marquee events and wedding
receptions contact the Catering
Manager ☎ (0532) 886101.
Dogs: So long as they are kept on a
lead, dogs are welcome in the
grounds but not in the House or
Bird Garden.

Harrogate
Harlow Carr Botanical Gardens
Cragg Lane, on B1612 to
Beckwithshaw (off Otley Road)
68 acres of gardens
☎ (0423) 565418
Open: daily 9am-7.30pm or dusk.

Harrogate International Festival
Wide ranging programme of
events including concerts, opera,
drama etc. Details from the Festival
Office, Royal Baths, Harrogate,
HG1 2RR ☎ (0423) 562303

Harrogate Theatre
Box Office ☎ (0423) 502116

Royal Pump Room Museum
Crown Place
Harrogate HG1 2RY
☎ (0423) 503340
Open: April to end of October
10am-5pm Monday to Saturday 2-
5pm. November to end March.
Monday to Saturday 10am-4pm.
Sunday 2-4pm.

Knaresborough

Ye Old Chymist Shoppe
16 Market Place ☎ (0423) 863153

Knaresborough Castle
Home of the Plantagenet Kings of
England. Fourteenth-century court
house adjacent. ☎ (0423) 503340
Open: Easter then late spring to
end of September.

Ripley

Ripley Castle and Gardens
Home of the Ingilby family for over
600 years, 3 miles (5km) north of
Harrogate.
☎ (0423) 770152
Open: April, May, October, Saturday and Sunday 11.30am-4.30pm.
June to September daily except Monday and Friday, 11.30am-4.30pm.

Ripon

Adam House and Gardens
☎ (0423) 322583
Open: daily except Mondays (but
including Bank Holidays),
Easter to end of September, from 11am.

Fountains Abbey and Studley Royal
3 miles (5km) south-west of Ripon.
Largest monastic ruin in Britain,
maintained by National Trust.
Open: April to June and September
daily 10am-7pm; July to August
daily 10am-8pm; October to March
daily, except Christmas Eve and
Christmas Day, 10am-4pm.

Newby Hall and Gardens
☎ (0423) 322583
Open: daily except Mondays (but
incl. Bank Holidays), Easter to end
of September, from 11am.

Skipton

Embassy Steam Railway
1½ miles of track
☎ (0756) 794727

Skipton Castle
Complete medieval castle
☎ (0756) 792442
Open: all year, except Christmas
Day, from 10am (Sunday 2pm).

Tourist Information Centres

Harrogate
Royal Baths Assembly Rooms
Crescent Road
Harrogate HG1 2RR
☎ (0423) 525666 Fax: (0423) 525669
Open: all year round.

Knaresborough
35 Market Place
☎ (0423) 866886
Open: April to mid-October.

Accommodation and Eating Out

A full list of accommodation is
available from the Harrogate
Tourist Information Centre which
also runs an accommodation
booking service.
The nearest hotel to Harewood
House is the Harewood Arms
Hotel, Harewood, near Leeds, LS17
9LH ☎ (0532) 886566. However this
is an upmarket hotel (Four Crowns,
English Tourist Board classifica-
tion) and therefore comparatively
expensive.
A list of accommodation in the
Yorkshire Dales National Park is
available from the National Park
Office.

Colvend
National Park Office
Hebden Road
Grassington
Skipton
North Yorks. B23 5LB
☎ (0756) 752748

8

CASTLE HOWARD

Approaching the house from the south, from York on the A64, one climbs up a narrow lane. Here a monument suddenly comes into view. It is the first notion that you are on the edge of a large estate. The significant column, erected in 1869, commemorates George William Frederick, seventh Earl of Carlisle, who had died in 1864. It stands on a large plinth with pedestals in each corner carved with heraldic shields and topped with coat of armour helmets carved in stone.

From here, the road proceeds between an avenue of trees in a straight line towards the first of two entrance arches. The first is the Carrmire Gate and is flanked by castellated walling and twin terminal towers. The second obelisk was raised in 1714 and is 100ft (30m) high. It conveniently disappears from view as you approach the Gatehouse with its curtain wall, eleven towers, bastions etc, enabling the eye to wander along the imposing ediface. Unfortunately, parts of the walling have collapsed and await restoration.

The wings to the gate were erected in 1756 to accommodate visitors to the house. In fact the latter has been open to visitors ever since it was built. If you pull up having gone through the Gatehouse archway and look to the right there is a fine view across the 1,000-acre park to the Mausoleum. It is possible to see the dome on the house peeping through the trees. Both are tasters of the spectacle to come!

Upon reaching the obelisk turn right down the drive. The car park is immediately on your right adjacent to the old stable block built by John Carr of York and now housing the visitors' entrance to the estate and the Costume Galleries. A visit in springtime is rewarded by the views of thousands of daffodils planted around the park.

Between 1979 and 1980, the TV series *Brideshead Revisited* was filmed at Castle Howard. This had a significant impact upon the house, increasing its popularity and equally importantly, its revenue. Even now, there is a steady stream of visitors who come here as a result of the series, including many American visitors. The film is available on a three-video pack available in the house shop.

Standing facing the south front of Castle Howard, one's eye can be momentarily overwhelmed by the elegance of the vista. However if one strips away the east and west wings together with the dome, the central core is very reminiscent of Chatsworth's west front. There are nine bays on each house divided by pilasters which rest on a rusticated lower course. Both have a decorated frieze with a balustrade above supporting urns and broken by a carved pediment. Even the central window below the pediment is flanked by garlands on each house.

The Chatsworth west front was built between 1700 and 1703, after William Talman, the architect, had been dismissed in 1696. Although the design of the Chatsworth front has been attributed to various people, it is possible that previous work by Talman had an influence upon the design. Talman had been retained at Castle Howard too, but he was similarly dismissed from his commission in 1699. He was replaced by Sir John Vanbrugh who, tantalisingly, had also been at Chatsworth for four or five days in 1699. Did Vanbrugh have an influence on the design of both houses rather than Talman, or was he influenced by the Chatsworth designs? This still remains a mystery.

The story of Castle Howard began earlier, in 1693 when Henderskelfe Castle was destroyed by fire. It was only ten years after the castle had been rebuilt. The owner, Charles Howard, third Earl of Carlisle decided to rebuild on a nearby site. We can only speculate why the Earl turned to Vanbrugh, a fellow member of the Kit-Cat Club, who had little training as an architect. The result was remarkable. At that time, the conventional approach was to orientate the building on a north-south axis, facing east and west. Vanbrugh built Castle Howard facing north and south, taking advantage of the views in each direction.

The central block, dome and east wing took fourteen years to complete, being finished in 1714. The dome was the first example to be incorporated into a private house and Vanbrugh was clearly influenced by St Paul's Cathedral and the domes at Greenwich Hospital. At Chatsworth, the Great Hall, later the Painted Hall, lay in a separate wing beyond the courtyard from the entrance wing. Here at Castle Howard the Great Hall encompasses virtually the whole of the building between the north and south fronts. It has a 52ft (15m) square floor and rises 70ft (21m) to the dome. It is breathtaking even today, looking more like the interior of a Baroque cathedral than a domestic house. In the early years of the eighteenth century it was revolutionary!

Vanbrugh was assisted by Nicholas Hawksmoor who was assistant architect to Sir Christopher Wren and had been associated with the work at St Pauls and Greenwich Hospital. Much of the detail at Castle Howard resulted from Hawksmoor working closely with Vanbrugh. In fact some later developments were his responsibility completely, such as the Mausoleum. Hawksmoor was in fact an architect of the Government Board of Works, like Vanbrugh. It is fantastic to think that Castle Howard was the latter's first house.

It had been Vanbrugh's intention to construct a west wing but this had not been completed by the time of his death in 1726. A large forecourt on the north side, enclosed by a curtain wall and huge central gateway was built but had been removed by about 1770. Additional planned wings would have resulted in an overall length of nearly 670ft (204m) for the north front — a length that would have made the house the longest country house in England.

Work did in fact continue after 1726 and by 1737, the Earl had spent £78,000 on the house, the garden, plantations and 'outworks'. All the State Rooms were of moderate dimensions, despite the hugh size of the Great Hall. They all faced south (like Chatsworth) and Vanbrugh was pleased to announce that 'with moderate fires (they) are ovens'!

The house was still without its west wing and the fourth Earl was persuaded by his brother-in-law, Sir Thomas Robinson, an amateur architect, to allow him to finish the job. Robinson did not build the wing in sympathy with the east side of the house. In fact he lengthened the south front to accommodate a much wider wing. This work was done between 1753 and 1759. A rather nice bow window with twin cupolas on the roof was removed during this building work, which was more in the fashionable Palladian style than work of Vanbrugh and Hawksmoor. It included the Long Gallery and Chapel. Robinson was an amateur architect but eventually prevailed upon the fourth Earl to allow him to make the alterations. The Earl did not like the result and Robinson's ideas for altering the east side of the house came to nothing in any event, with the death of the Earl.

His successor did little to the west wing other than provide a roof. His gambling interests preoccupied him at the expense of the house. However around 1800, the interior was completed by C.H. Tatham. Further work was undertaken in the nineteenth century by the ninth Earl when an attic storey at each end of the wing was removed in an attempt to harmonise the roof levels. Alterations to the chapel were also made together with the extension of the north front steps around the west wing.

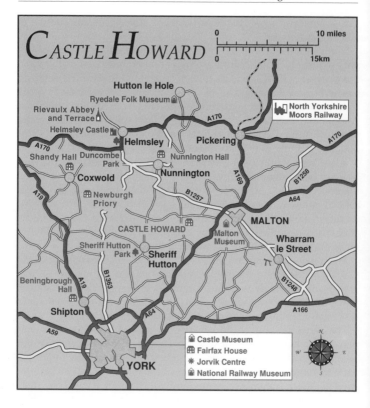

The outer buildings to the east broadly followed the Vanbrugh scheme and it is possible to imagine how the house would have looked if his west wing had been built. Simply imagine the west side as a mirror image of the east. The change meant that a fresh plan had to be drawn up for the stables and this was done by John Carr of York in between 1781 and 1784. Coincidentally, the link with Chatsworth repeats itself once more, for at this time, the Duke of Devonshire was building The Crescent at Buxton, also designed by Carr, and the first imitation of the famous Crescent at Bath.

The layout of the park did however follow Vanbrugh's design. The walled garden's Satyr Gate dates from 1705 for instance, but not everything was completed prior to his death. Vanbrugh laid out the South Lake in 1724 for instance but the New River and Bridge dates from the 1730s and 1740s and the Cascade and the Waterfalls date from the early 1860s.

Springtime at Castle Howard

With the outbreak of World War II the house was occupied as a girls' school by Queen Margaret's School of Scarborough. During their occupation, fire broke out in the south-east wing on 9 November 1940. The blaze gutted the whole of the wing and nearly twenty rooms were lost. It also consumed the cupola and the lantern of the dome, the Garden Hall (between the Great Hall and the south front) and the first of the State Rooms adjacent. Pellegrini murals including his work on the dome ceiling were lost as molten lead poured down onto the Hall floor. School girls helped in the removal of as much of the furnishings as could be salvaged by many local people who responded to the house's hour of need. Daylight on the following day revealed just what had been lost. The south-east wing was completely destroyed. Only the walls survived. The intense heat had even consumed the plasterwork. The dome had collapsed into a heap of charred beams and embers on the Great Hall floor. All the windows on the central south front, let alone the south-east wing had gone too. Fortunately a lot of the furniture and paintings had been put into storage for the duration of the War and were saved as a result. In 1960 the dome was recreated and in 1962 Scott Medd, a Canadian artist, was employed to recreate the picture of *The Fall of Phaeton* which Pellegrini had painted 250 years previously.

After World War II, it was not expected that the family would occupy the house again and the Trustees had opened negotiations with the school for the sale of the house. However George Howard decided to return and set about its restoration. He had the dome rebuilt and many of the principal rooms have been refurbished. The south-east wing, despite being roofed over, remains a shell. In recent times, noticeable improvements by George Howard's son Hon. Simon Howard has seen the restoration of the waterworks to the south of the house, the development of the cafeteria by the Great Lake and the planting programme in Ray Wood. Several of the monuments have also been restored, including the Temple of the Four Winds in the 1950s and the Mausoleum in the 1970s.

A tour of the house begins in the west wing, where a flight of stairs is taken up to the first floor. On the left is a bust of the sixth Duke of Devonshire and a considerable amount of fine china, including Crown Derby, Meissen, Chelsea and Minton housed in a superb eighteenth-century cabinet.

The blue ceramic ware above the cabinet is Chinese and also eighteenth century except for the middle one which is early seventeenth century. In the cabinet is a group of Crown Derby dinner ware painted yellow. The application of the yellow paint caused such illness among the decorators that no second set was made.

The route through the first floor shows some of the south front furniture which had been stored and thereby saved from the fire. The first room however contains the **bedroom** furniture of Lady Georgiana Cavendish, the sister of the sixth Duke of Devonshire, who married George Howard, the sixth Earl of Carlisle. It is furnished as it was when she died in 1858. She was the daughter of Georgiana Spencer, the Regency socialite who married the fifth Duke of Devonshire, and who was a prodigious party giver, gambler and curiously, happy to live with her husband and his mistress. She is portrayed on a print of the famous Chatsworth painting of her by Reynolds along with her baby daughter after whom this room is named. The four-poster bed dates from around 1770. The room also has a Louis XV bureau and a Rudd's dressing table. In the eighteenth century clothes were kept in clothes presses and there is one here.

The next room is **Lady Georgiana's Dressing Room**. Look for the portrait of Blanche, Georgiana's daughter. It is on the right as you enter the room and Blanche is portrayed in a red dress. Like her grandmother, she married into the Cavendish family but she unfortunately died before her husband William became the seventh Duke of Devonshire, a loss from which he never recovered. She was only 28 years old. Despite this, Georgiana was to see her family grow substantially for she had twelve children in all.

Visitors to Chatsworth may recall the latin inscription on the fireplace in the Painted Hall. It states that William Spencer had inherited the house in 1811 and finished it 'in the year of his breavement, 1840'. This relates to the loss of his beloved niece, Blanche. The painting opposite the one of Blanche shows her daughter. The room now houses a four-poster bed, recent addition.

The next room was also a dressing room. The bed (formerly in the State Rooms of the south-east wing) was used by Queen Victoria when she stayed here. The room after that, was the bedroom to Lady Georgiana's husband, the sixth Earl, who used the latter room from 1825 to1848. It is now known as the **Castle Howard Bedroom**. The bedroom has recently been completely renovated. The furniture is chiefly eighteenth century although the German chest is a little older. Much of the furniture is by John Linnel and the paintings are by Marco Ricci.

After leaving this bedroom, one walks down the **Antique Passage**, lined with statuary. Much of it was collected by the fourth Earl and reflects the early taste for such things, although some pieces are still pleasing to view. The sixth Earl collected statuary too, being influenced by his uncle, the fifth Duke of Devonshire, another avid statuary collector. The passage brings one to the Great Hall.

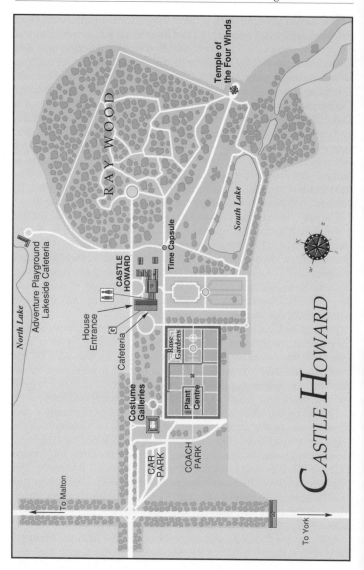

CASTLE HOWARD

One needs to stand in the **Great Hall** for some time just to absorb it all. Have regard to the fact that this was the first time such a feature was created in a house in England. It is broadly reminiscent of the dome in St Paul's Cathedral, which precedes it by perhaps a little over a decade. The hall is 70ft (21m) high and only 52ft (15m) across but this is successfully overcome. The walls dividing the adjacent stairwells are pierced and this creates a feeling of greater spaciousness. Opposite the fireplace a niche contains a second century AD

Crown Derby: Botanical dessert service

Lady Georgiana's Bedroom

sculpture of Bacchus and there are another four sculptures, one in each corner of the hall. Two females face north and the males face south. The females are Hygeia (second century AD) and a Roman Empress as Ceres (second to third century AD). The males are Augustus Caesar (first century AD) and Aurelius Caesar (third century AD).

Take a good look at Nadauld's carving of the capitals to the Corinthian-style columns and the acanthus leaf brackets supporting the underside of the balcony on the south side at first floor level, which were carved by Samuel Carpenter. Above the arches, the walls are painted and portray The Elements, Apollo and various other mythological subjects. They are the work of Antonio Pellegrini and fortunately survived the fire.

Look too at the intricate iron work on the balcony balustrade and in the dome. You can see more on the stairs either side of the Hall. It is the work of John Gardam, a Derbyshire man who also worked at Windsor Castle and Chatsworth. Unfortunately he died early, in 1713 at the age of 48 years. He was buried at Baslow near Chatsworth.

The **Garden Hall** was destroyed in the fire. It is a large, pleasant and uncluttered room. After all the intricate carving, iron work and decoration in the Great Hall, the Garden Hall offers a pleasing contrast. The previous decoration by Pellegrini has not been recreated here; the painted panels are recent and portray imaginary Vanbrugh buildings. The view from its windows are down to the Atlas fountain, purchased after the Great Exhibition of 1851. Off to the left is the south-east wing which awaits restoration. The tour turns to the right towards the west wing. The rooms are enfiladed and the eye is drawn towards a Delft tulip vase framed by the bay window of the Museum Room.

The first room was the most westerly room destroyed by fire. The walls are lined with fabric and the room is used for displays. Moving through, one reaches the **Music Room**. It has two pianos, both by Broadwood. The larger one dates from 1796 costing £30 and was used by Lady Georgiana. The smaller, square piano is a little later, dating from 1805. Both are in very good condition. Take a good look at the walls and frieze. Everything is made of pinewood and not plaster. The Tapestry Room adjacent is the same. They were carved by Nadauld and the aptly-named Samuel Carpenter. The small harp is of the same period and perhaps was used to teach children. The china is Meissen and Coalport. The globe must be fairly early; it shows Tasmania attached to Australia! The paintings include a Gainsborough and the maghogany elbow chairs date from about 1750.

The **Tapestry Room** is named after the tapestries of the four seasons which were removed at the time of the fire and await restoration. There are four paintings here by Reynolds and yet another by Gainsborough. The large mahogany table was cut from one piece of wood and it is particularly well grained. It is one of a pair, but the other is not on show. The dining chairs are part of a set of twenty and the baby's high chair is by Chippendale. Note the Roman mosaic table as you leave the room. It sits on an eighteenth-century frame and is one of several. Others may be seen in the Antique Passage. The inner door is off-centre to accommodate one of the tapestries. The carving over the door might be by Grinling Gibbons. House accounts indicate that he was paid for work here but nothing survives which may be attributed to him with certainty.

The room has a cellarette inlaid with four different woods, used for keeping red wine at room temperature, and two triangular plate cupboards flanking a side table.

The **Orleans Room** is next. It takes its name from the collection of paintings purchased by Frederick the fifth Earl of Carlisle in the late eighteenth century from the collection of the Duc d'Orleans. Some of those paintings still hang here augmented by others, including one by Rubens of the head of John the Baptist.

The end room was altered by Robinson, losing its large bow at the end of the wing when he built the west wing to a wider plan than the east wing. It destroyed the symmetry of the north and south fronts as well as altering the roof line. The Museum Room opens onto the Long Gallery and is full of curios and relics. There is a painting of George, the ninth Earl (and last one to reside here, for the estate was subsequently split and the tenth Earl inherited Naworth Castle in Cumbria). The ninth Earl was a good artist and several of his works hang here. The Delft tulip vase dates from the late seventeenth century and is made in five parts. It sits on a William Kent table of 1735. There is a rare Derbyshire Blue John table, about 30in (76cm) in diameter. Amongst the curios are two small wheel barrows presented to the seventh Earl upon the opening of two railways in Southern Ireland in the 1850s.

The **Long Gallery**, started in 1750 and finished in 1810 extends down most of the length of the west front. It is divided into three by the Octagon, the roof of which so strongly emphasises the difference in styles of the west and east wings. The Octagon contains two Holbeins which recall the influence the Howards once enjoyed at Court. The paintings are of Henry VIII and Thomas Howard, third Duke of Norfolk and uncle to Queen Anne Boleyn and Queen Katherine Howard. Howard fell from grace however following the

The Great Hall, Vanbrugh's splendid architectural creation

The Antique Passage, yet another of Vanbrugh's innovations

execution of both Queens. The Long Gallery was originally used by ladies of the house for taking exercise. Now it accommodates a significant number of paintings and is used for special events. It may also be hired for corporate hospitality, weddings etc.

Formerly, the room was followed on the same level by the Chapel, but this was lowered in the late nineteenth century. This certainly gave the room a greater sense of proportion, but the access down and then back up a succession of steps detracts from the overall scheme. The **Chapel** itself is richly decorated and is all the more striking for its Corinthian columns at either end of the room. The stained-glass windows are panels inset inside the plain-glass windows. The stained glass was designed by Burne-Jones and manufactured by William Morris between 1870 and 1875. The future ninth Earl was a friend of many of the Pre Raphaelites.

Behind the font, on the right as you enter the Chapel is a plaster bas-relief of the Madonna and Child. It is by Sansovino (1460-1529) and is an important feature in the collection.

From the Chapel, steps lead down to the shop, café and exit. This is not the end of the tour of the house, however, for the south-east wing may also be visited. Still ruined by the fire, one can enter the wing at the far end of the south front. Notices describe detail of the former rooms and by using photographs of complimentary scenes in the south-west wing (eg the main staircase in the wing) one can visualise how things would have looked. A modern staircase gives access to the first floor level where there are displays on the fire and on the restoration work in the Park.

The landscaping of the **Park** was an integral part of the overall design of the house. The Parterre to the south of the house has been redesigned at least twice since the original concept, but important features in the Park are intact. These include the **Temple of the Four Winds** and the **Mausoleum**. The former was designed by Vanbrugh between 1724 and 1726. It is domed and has four Ionic porticoes. It was Vanbrugh's last work before he died. Together with the Mausoleum the two buildings have been described as probably the most beautiful landscape buildings in Europe.

Both buildings have been restored; the interior of the Temple was virtually beyond repair and the dome is new, having been made in a craftsman's workshop, cut into quarters and then reassembled on site. The Mausoleum was designed by Nicholas Hawksmoor for the third Earl and was completed in 1743. It is the largest private mausoleum in western Europe. It is 90ft (27m) high and has a total of twenty columns. The restoration work involved the dismantling of each column one by one. Eroded or cracked stone was replaced and the centre of the columns filled with grout to bond the stones together. Although the main structure is now safe, work is still needed on the balustrading and steps.

One building which collapsed prior to restoration was the **Temple of Venus**, also designed by Hawksmoor. It was unusual in that it had an octagonal design. It was situated in Ray Wood. Only the base now survives, but the statue of Venus may still be seen, now relocated in the Rose Garden.

The work of restoration continues apace, but it is enormously expensive. Fortunately, the popularity associated with *Brideshead Revisited* brings many additional visitors. In November 1991, additional working capital was raised by a sale of unwanted furnishings. Sotheby's conducted the auction over three days and there were 1,636 lots, it raised approximately £2 million pounds. Already the impact of this can be seen in the refurbishment of the Castle Howard Bedroom and restoration of the paintings.

The waterworks below the south lake have been restored in recent years. The Cascade and Waterfall can be seen running along with the Prince of Wales Fountain. The ponds on the south side of the **Great Lake**, long silted up, have been cleared too. A lakeside café is on the Great Lake and boat trips in a Victorian-style boat are an additional feature in summer months. The ultimate goal is the restoration of the south-east wing. It is over fifty years since the fire and certainly the last decade has seen great strides in all manner of detail.

There are two other attractions here which have been established since World War II: the **Costume Galleries** and the replanting of Ray Wood. The Galleries, founded in 1965, contain the largest private collection of eighteenth- to twentieth-century costume in Britain.

The collection includes examples of domestic ecclesiastical, occupational, theatrical and military clothing. It has over 140 costumes from the Diaghilev Russian Ballet and there are many examples of coronation and court dress, mourning, hats, shoes, underwear etc. The Galleries also has an excellent replica set of the Crown Jewels.

Ray Wood was felled during World War II and replanted in 1946. Thirty years later it was decided to create an amenity woodland. Some of the timber was removed and today this 30-acre woodland garden has an important collection of rare trees, rhododendrons, azaleas, bamboo, and hydrangeas from around the world. Three seasonal leaflets are on sale together with an accession list (available from the Curator of the Arboreta). There are specialist guided tours available for party bookings although there is a minimum of twelve persons. The extensive Rose Gardens contain a considerable number of different species and there is an extensive plant centre.

The Long Gallery

Hawksmoor's Mausoleum, one of the most magnificent landscaped buildings in Europe

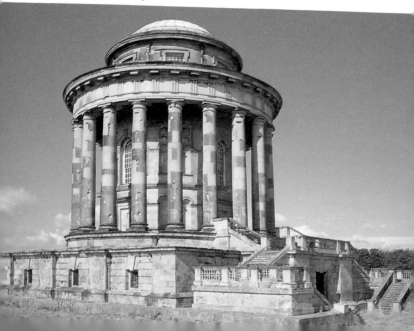

The Temple of the Four Winds sat comfortably upon its promontory with the Mausoleum in the distance

A colourful array of plants in Ray Wood

Attractions Around Castle Howard

Castle Howard is situated in an Area of Outstanding Natural Beauty just to the south of the Howardian Hills, a low range to the south of the **North Yorkshire Moors National Park**. The latter is an area of spectacular beauty. In spring, some of its valleys such as Farn Dale lie beneath carpets of daffodils. In the autumn, the moors turn purple as the heather comes into flower. To the south is **York**, one of the most important historical cities in Britain, with its Roman, Viking and later periods of history. Even its name York reflects its Viking connection — they called it Jorvik. The area around Castle Howard has many interesting backwaters and quiet lanes down which you may wander with your car. Beyond the nearby market town of Malton are several large country houses, ruined abbeys (including the spectacular remains of Rievaulx Abbey) and the quiet and simple beauty of Rievaulx Terrace. Perhaps the most enigmatic of all the historic places in the Howardian Hills district is the deserted medieval village of Wharram Percy at Wharram-le-Street.

To get there, take the B1248 North Grimston road for about 7 miles (11km) to **Wharram-le-Street** and then take the next metalled lane on the right. It is rather narrow and just beyond Bella Farm there is a car park. From here take a track into the valley. It crosses a stream and former railway line. Bear to the left and continue onto the site of the village marked by undulations in the fields. The church remains, though ruined, and this can be seen if the track is followed further beyond some cottages.

Remains from the prehistoric to the medieval period have been found in the various excavations which began in 1952. There was a village here in Saxon times and it is believed this was situated near to the church which was built in late Saxon times. In the twelfth century, expansion of the village saw fresh development away from the stream. The manor house was separated away from the houses with a village green between. Further development in the next century saw an extension of village houses towards the manor house, which itself was then relocated further to the north.

Excavations have revealed corn-drying kilns and the presence of a corn mill. The church was enlarged and then reduced in size before the village became abandoned, probably as people moved to find work elsewhere. Most of the church tower remains intact, but much of the church is roofless, despite the walls being to eaves height.

Although further away, to the north this time, a visit to **Helmsley** is well worth while. It is an old market town and has a castle with a unique D-shaped keep. It was erected between 1186 and 1227 but was beseiged by Parliamentary forces under Sir Thomas Fairfax during the Civil War. Fairfax destroyed much of the castle, but the remains are substantial nonetheless. It is situated on the western side of the town.

Nearby are the remains of **Rievaulx Abbey**, built by the Cistercian monks in the twelfth century. The abbey church remains are substantial and well worth a visit. Above the abbey, high on the hillside is Rievaulx Terrace, now owned by the National Trust. There are two temples here, one Ionic and the other Tuscan in design and built in the eighteenth century. The site was levelled and the buildings erected by Thomas Duncombe of Duncombe Park. There are views down to the abbey and the terrace makes an ideal picnic spot, especially when the spring flowers are in bloom on the bankside below the lawned terrace.

South of Helmsley is **Duncombe Park**. It has recently returned to domestic use after being a girls' school for many years. A terrace walk with Ionic temple leads to Helmsley Castle. It was intended to link it to Rievaulx Terrace, but the work was never completed. Duncombe Park is now open for visitors once more and has extensive gardens and parkland.

Nearer to Castle Howard are one or two other attractions worth visiting. **Nunnington Hall** is now owned by the National Trust and is to be found just to the north of the Howardian Hills. It is a large seventeenth-century manor house and is noted for its collection of twenty-two miniature rooms which are designed in different architectural styles. Part of the house is older, dating from the sixteenth century. The house boasts a magnificent panelled hall and carved fireplace. There are several panelled bedrooms and displays of fine tapestries and china. The house is situated on the banks of the River Wye

Looking down on Rievaulx Abbey from Rievaulx Terrace

The Ionic Temple at Rievaulx Terrace

Additional Information

Places to Visit

Castle Howard

Open: daily from March until
October from 11am (Grounds from
10am).
Directions: Castle Howard is
situated to the north of the A64.
Some 10 miles (6km) north-east of
York a signposted road to the left
goes northwards to the house.
Alternatively the A61 may be taken
from the A1 via Thirsk and up
Sutton Bank on the A170. At
Sproxton, where the A170 turns
sharply to the left to enter
Helmsley, take the B1257 to
Slingsby and then turn south to the
house. The nearest train stations
are York and Malton.

Services and Information
Contact Castle Howard,
Coneysthorpe, York YO6 7DA
☎ 065 384333
Private tours of the house are
available at additional cost. They
take place at 10am and last 1 ¼
hours. Parties are met at the north
front by the Administrator and
taken on a tour of the house by a
specially selected guide. Different
specialists are available upon
request for specific interests.
Guests stop in the Great Hall for a
Brideshead Cocktail or coffee
before proceeding further. When
the Hon. Mrs Simon Howard is at
home she is always happy to join
the party. The charge is inclusive of
the Costume Galleries.

Adventure Playgrounds
There are two; one by the lakeside tearoom and the other between the Plant Centre and the Costume Galleries.

Special Events
There are a series of special events held during the summer. Telephone the house for full details.

Fishing
Tickets are available for the 71-acre Great Lake for every day between 16 June and 17 March. Bream, tench, roach, perch and pike can all be found in the lake. Full details are available from the Fishing Bailiff, North Lodge, Coneysthorpe, York YO6 7DH ☎ 065 384331

Corporate Hospitality and Country-House Entertaining
There is a long tradition of hospitality and entertaining at Castle Howard. Today this takes the form of banquets, receptions, clay-pigeon shooting, trade presentations, wine tasting, wedding receptions etc. The Promotions Manager is happy to discuss your requirements.

Coxwold
Newburgh Priory
Coxwold, York
The house dates from 1145 and has a history of association with one family, one of whom married the daughter of Oliver Cromwell, whose headless remains were reburied here. Parkland, large rock garden and café.
☎ 0347 6435
Open: April to end June, house and grounds Wednesday and Sunday 2-6pm. July and August grounds only Wednesday and Sunday 2-6pm. Parties at other times by arrangement. For entrance to the grounds only, children enter free of charge.

Shandy Hall
The Laurence Sterne Trust
Shandy Hall
Coxwold, York YO6 4AD
A 500-year-old house where Laurence Sterne wrote *Tristram Shandy* and *A Sentimental Journey* in the eighteenth century. Walled gardens with many unusual plants.
☎ 0347 6465
Open: June to September 2-4.30pm. Sundays 2.30-4.30pm.

Helmsley
Duncombe Park
Near Helmsley
York YO6 5EB
House dates from 1713 but remodelled after a major fire in late nineteenth century. Unique early eighteenth-century landscaped garden with temples, terraces etc, waymarked walks, tearoom and shop.
☎ 0439 70213
Open: April, Sundays plus all Easter weekend. May to October open Sundays to Thursdays, plus Saturdays prior to Bank Holidays 11am-6pm.

Hutton-le-Hole
Ryedale Folk Museum
York YO6 6UA
Yorkshire's leading open-air museum. Twelve buildings in 2½ acres, including Elizabethan Manor House, oldest photographic studio in Britain, craft buildings etc.
☎ 0751 5367
Open: April to end October daily 10am-5.30pm. Last admission 4.30pm.

Kirkham Priory
Near Whitwell on the Hill, south-west of Malton
Thirteenth-century gatehouse situated in a riverside setting.
Open: mid-March to mid-October, weekdays 9.30am-6.30pm, Sundays 2-6pm. October to March, week-days 9.30am-4pm, Sundays 2-4pm.

Malton
Malton Museum
Old Town Hall
Market Place
North Yorkshire YO17 0LT
Imaginative displays of Roman remains. Lively programme of exhibitions and events.
☎ 0653 695136
Open: Easter Saturday to end of October. Monday to Saturday 10am-4pm. Sunday 2-4pm.

Nunnington
Nunnington Hall
Near Helmsley
York YO6 5UY
Large seventeenth-century manor house. Carlisle collection of miniature rooms furnished in period style. Owned by National Trust. ☎ 043 95 283
Open: April to October, Tuesday, Wednesday, Thursday, Saturday and Good Friday (Easter) 2-6pm. Fridays, July and August only. Sundays and Bank Holidays 12noon-6pm. Last admission 5pm. Tearoom and shop.

Pickering
North Yorkshire Moors Railway
Pickering Station
Pickering YO18 7AJ
Steam railway.
☎ 0751 73535
Open: daily mid-February to October (excluding March — Sundays only).

Rievaulx
Rievaulx Abbey
Near Helmsley
Yorkshire
Substantial remains of former abbey.
☎ 0439 6228
Open: daily.

Rievaulx Terrace
Rievaulx
Helmsley, Yorks YO6 5LJ
Two mid-eighteenth-century temples on a ½ mile long terrace above Rievaulx Abbey. National Trust.
☎ 0439 96340
Open: 1 April to 31 October daily 10.30am-6pm. Last admissions 5pm. Ionic temple closed 1-2pm. Shop and Information Centre.

Sheriff Hutton
Sheriff Hutton Park
Sheriff Hutton, York YO6 1RH
A seventeenth-century mansion relatively undiscovered. Gardens and walks in wooded park.
☎ 034 77 442
Open: Monday to Friday 10am-4.30pm. Closed mid-December to mid-January.

Shipton by Beningbrough
Beningbrough Hall
York YO6 1DD
An early Georgian country house with much exceptional wood carving. Houses over 100 eight-eenth-century portraits on loan from the National Portrait Gallery. Restaurant and shop plus 7 acres of garden. National Trust.
☎ 0904 470666
Open: April to September, Mondays, Tuesdays, Wednesdays, Saturdays, Good Friday. Also Fridays in July and August.

House opens: 11am-5pm. Last admissions 4.30pm.
Grounds, shop and restaurant: 11am-5.30pm. Last admissions 5pm.

York

Castle Museum
☎ 0904 653611
Open: daily from 9.30am Monday to Saturday. Sunday from 10am. Last admission 5.30pm. Museum by 6.15pm. Closed Christmas Day, Boxing Day and New Years Day.

Fairfax House
Castlegate
☎ 0904 655543
Classical Georgian house and furniture.
Open: March to January, Monday to Saturday 11am-5pm. Closed Friday. Sunday 1.30-5pm.

Jorvik Viking Centre
Coppergate
☎ 0904 643211
Open: daily April to October, 9am-7pm; November to March, 9am-5.30pm. Evening viewing for parties of at least fifty from 7 or 7.30pm. No party reductions.

National Railway Museum
Leeman Road
☎ 0904 621261
Open: weekdays 10am-6pm, Sunday 11am-6pm; Closed Good Friday, Christmas Eve, Christmas Day, Boxing Day, New Years Day.

Tourist Information Centres

A free holiday information pack on Ryedale may be obtained from Ryedale Tourism, Ryedale House, Malton, North Yorkshire YO17

0HH ☎ 0653 600666. A local bed booking service is also available. There are tourist information centres in the following nearby towns:

Helmsley
Market Place
☎ 0439 70173

Malton
Market Place
☎ 0653 600048

Pickering
Eastgate Car Park
☎ 0751 73791

Accommodation

See comment above on the local bed booking service. A booklet — *Ryedale Where to Stay* gives a full list of local accommodation, including farm houses and self catering. It is available from Ryedale Tourism.
Farmhouse bed and breakfast on a working dairy farm close to Castle Howard is available at Gate Farm, Ganthorpe, Terrington, York YO6 4QD.
☎ 0653 84269.

Castle Howard
Castle Howard Estate Ltd has a caravan site. It has 122 static caravans and facilities for 40 tents and 40 caravans. It is within walking distance and sight of Castle Howard, adjacent to the Great Lake. Coarse fishing is available. Write to the Caravan Site Manager at Coneysthorpe, York YO6 7DA.
☎ 0653 84366

INDEX

Page numbers in **bold** type indicate maps

Reduced Admission Vouchers

Beaulieu   **VOUCHER**

With this Voucher you will obtain one adult admission at child rate,
if accompanied by at least one person paying full adult rate.
Not available when party rates or other concessions apply.

Broadlands   **VOUCHER**

With this Voucher you will obtain one adult admission at child rate,
if accompanied by at least one person paying full adult rate.
Not available when party rates or other concessions apply.

Woburn Abbey   **VOUCHER**

With this Voucher you will obtain one adult admission at child rate,
if accompanied by at least one person paying full adult rate.
Not available when party rates or other concessions apply.

Blenheim Palace   **VOUCHER**

With this Voucher you will obtain one adult admission at child rate,
if accompanied by at least one person paying full adult rate.
Not available when party rates or other concessions apply.

Warwick Castle   **VOUCHER**

With this Voucher you will obtain one adult admission at child rate,
if accompanied by at least one person paying full adult rate.
Not available when party rates or other concessions apply.

Chatsworth   **VOUCHER**

With this Voucher you will obtain one adult admission at child rate,
if accompanied by at least one person paying full adult rate.
Not available when party rates or other concessions apply.

Harewood House   **VOUCHER**

With this Voucher you will obtain one adult admission at child rate,
if accompanied by at least one person paying full adult rate.
Not available when party rates or other concessions apply.

Castle Howard   **VOUCHER**

With this Voucher you will obtain one adult admission at child rate,
if accompanied by at least one person paying full adult rate.
Not available when party rates or other concessions apply.